NORTON OF EVEREST

NORTON OF EVEREST

The biography of E.F. Norton, soldier and mountaineer

Hugh Norton

FOREWORD BY WADE DAVIS

Published by Vertebrate Publishing, Sheffield.
www.v-publishing.co.uk

NORTON OF EVEREST

The biography of E.F. Norton,
soldier and mountaineer

Hugh Norton

First published in 2017 by Vertebrate Publishing.

VP Vertebrate Publishing
Crescent House, 228 Psalter Lane, Sheffield S11 8UT UK.
www.v-publishing.co.uk

This book is a work of non-fiction based on the life, experiences and recollections of Hugh Norton. In some limited cases the names of people, places, dates and sequences or the detail of events have been changed solely to protect the privacy of others. The author has stated to the publishers that, except in such minor respects not affecting the substantial accuracy of the work, the contents of the book are true.

A CIP catalogue record for this book is available from the British Library.

ISBN: 978-1-910240-92-2 (Paperback)
ISBN: 978-1-910240-93-9 (Ebook)

VP Design and production by Nathan Ryder.
Vertebrate Publishing – www.v-publishing.co.uk

Vertebrate Publishing is committed to printing on paper from sustainable sources.

MIX
Paper from
responsible sources
FSC
www.fsc.org   FSC® C013056

Printed and bound in the UK by T.J. International Ltd, Padstow, Cornwall.

CONTENTS

FOREWORD

The epic story of the first British attempts on Everest in 1921–1924 has long been dominated by the charismatic figure of George Mallory, whose tragic and mysterious death on the final assault in 1924 secured his place in the firmament of Himalayan mountaineering. As the only climber to participate in all three early expeditions Mallory certainly deserves the recognition, but he was most assuredly not alone on the mountain. Altogether some twenty-five other climbers shared the great adventure. They were mostly but not exclusively British. The 1921 reconnaissance included Oliver Wheeler, a Canadian who actually found the route to the North Col, a discovery long attributed to Mallory. The 1922 expedition featured George Finch, an Australian by birth, who proved the efficacy of supplemental oxygen as he reached higher than anyone before him; had he not chosen to save the life of young Geoffrey Bruce he might well have reached the summit. The British contingent included the indomitable Howard Somervell who on his last attempt in 1924 coughed up the entire frost-scarred and bloody lining of his throat and simply kept walking. All of these men, along with their other climbing companions in 1921–1924, were extraordinary characters very much the equal of Mallory.

In recent years a number of books have been published, many by family members and descendants, which have finally given these climbers their due. Among the first of these books were two fine biographies of Sandy Wollaston and Henry Morshead, written by their sons, Nicholas Wollaston and Ian Morshead. Julie Summers wrote of her great uncle, Sandy Irvine, who perished with Mallory in 1924. Sandra Noel, daughter of the indefatigable John Noel, expedition filmmaker in 1922 and 1924, brought out a lovely collection of her father's photographs. Other books published recently or currently in the works revisit the contributions of George Finch, Oliver Wheeler, Arthur Wakefield and Richard Hingston, expedition physician in 1924.

But surely no account has been more eagerly anticipated than Hugh Norton's biography of his father, the incomparable Col. Edward Norton, who played a pivotal role in 1922 and served brilliantly as expedition leader in 1924. *Norton of Everest* is the perfect complement to *Everest Revealed: The Private Diaries and Sketches of Edward Norton, 1922–24*, an illustrated book of photographs and watercolours edited by Christopher Norton, grandson of the Colonel, nephew of Hugh, and first published in 2014. Indeed the entire Norton family including Hugh's brothers Dick and Bill have conspired in a marvellous way to give what can only be described as a literary gift to the mountaineering world.

Edward Felix 'Teddy' Norton, then thirty-eight, was the great discovery of the 1922 expedition, a man of extraordinary qualities of leadership, integrity, and grit. Commissioned as a graduate of the Royal Military Academy Woolwich in 1902, he had been a soldier since boyhood. Posted to Meerut at 22, he would over the years serve throughout India. While at Meerut, he became for a brief period aide-de-camp to the viceroy before sailing with his regiment to France in the late summer of 1914.

That he survived the war was a statistical miracle, for he fought in virtually every campaign, from the very first British attacks at Aisne and the Marne, through Ypres, Loos and the Somme, Arras and the German spring offensive of 1918. Mentioned in dispatches three times, he was awarded the Military Cross, appointed DSO, and honoured with every medal for gallantry and combat save the Victoria Cross.

Norton emerged from the war with a certain quality of being, a serenity, confidence and uncanny presence that caused men almost reflexively to follow his lead. 'Norton is one of the best,' George Mallory exclaimed to his beloved wife Ruth in his first reference to the new man, 'extraordinarily keen and active and full of interest and gentle and charming withal. He is to be my stable companion I understand and I don't doubt that I shall like him in that capacity as well as anyone.' Many months later when leadership on Everest in 1924 devolved to Norton, as fate inevitably would have it, one of the climbers marvelled how Norton as commander would make up his mind about a decision, then call in the entire expedition to confer. 'Invariably they would after discussion come to his view.'

In retrospect it was remarkable that Norton was even available to join the Everest effort. He had just passed through staff college and was destined for great things in the army. The Everest Committee had gone to the very top, Sir Henry Wilson, Chief of the Imperial General Staff, to secure for Norton eight months' leave, which Wilson granted in a letter of January 23, 1922. One senses the hand of Sir Francis Younghusband, then president of the Royal Geographical Society and a dominant figure in the entire Everest adventure, who perfectly distilled Norton's character and charisma in a brief biographical sketch:

'Major E. F. Norton, DSO, was well known in the Alpine Club and well versed in the lore of mountaineering. He had the additional advantage of having served in India and been on shooting expeditions in the Himalaya. He could speak Hindustani and knew how to handle Indian peoples. Compact and collected, erect and direct, and with a habit of command, he inspired confidence at once. And there was a kindliness and suavity about him, which increased the trust placed in him.

'He was indeed a combination of many qualities. As an officer of the Royal Horse Artillery he was noted for the smartness of his battery; he had served with distinction in the war; for seven years he had run the Kadir Cup Meeting – the great pig-sticking event in India; he was a keen observer of birds; and he was an amateur painter of more than average ability. In everything he was methodical … In his punctuality he took great pride: he would be neither too early nor too late. It was not much more than a minute before the train left Victoria that he arrived at the station on his way to India and he was leisurely saying goodbye to his friends and the train was well on the move as he quietly stepped into it continuing his conversation. With him there would be no flurry in emergency.'

In 1922 Norton proved exceptional in every way. Calm in crisis, stoic in the face of adversity, he was a confident leader whose measured orders were embraced readily by those under his command. Unlike so many of the senior officers the other climbers had all known during the war, Norton's mind did not run on rails. He was open to discussion, tolerant of debate, and had a way of making each man feel a part of what were ultimately his decisions alone. As a personality and a mountaineer he quite literally stood out from the pack. Mallory, Somervell, Geoffrey

Bruce, and indeed most of the alpine climbers, were of remarkably similar stature. Each was an inch shy of six feet and weighed roughly 160 pounds fully clothed. Norton by contrast was six foot four inches, exceedingly tall and thin, approximating, as he quipped, 'Euclid's definition of a straight line'. Heralded by all, and most especially by Mallory, Norton to the surprise of no one was selected as early as October 1922 to serve as climbing leader and second-in-command under General Charles Bruce for the 1924 expedition. When Bruce collapsed and had to be evacuated on the approach march from Darjeeling to Everest, leadership came naturally to the younger soldier.

Norton looms large over virtually every moment of the fateful expedition that would take the lives of George Mallory and Sandy Irvine, causing an entire war-torn nation to weep. He is perhaps best remembered by mountaineers for setting a height record as he struggled through the deep snow of the couloir that today bears his name on the north face of Everest. Others herald the calm and expedient manner in which he decisively rallied the survivors and abandoned the mountain in the wake of the tragedy. 'We were a sad little party,' Norton wrote on Monday 16 June 1924 as the expedition departed Rongbuk, 'and from the first we accepted the loss of our comrades in that rational spirit which all our generation had learnt in the Great War, and there was never any tendency to a morbid harping on the irrevocable. But the tragedy was very near. As so constantly in the war, so here in our mimic campaign death had taken his toll from the best.'

His greatest and most revealing act of leadership, however, occurred earlier in the 1924 expedition. Through a series of miscommunications, a group of native porters became stranded at 23,000 feet on the North Col. With the monsoon looming over the southern horizon, Norton knew that conditions could only worsen. If the porters were not rescued within the day, at most two, they would surely die. Yet after earlier mishaps the British climbers were exhausted, and their ordeal, the quest that had drawn them halfway around the world, had scarcely begun. Mallory and Somervell had bronchitis and terrible coughs from the altitude and cold. Irvine was down with diarrhoea. Noel Odell had not slept in days, and Jack Hazard with his seeping wound left over from the Somme was a nonstarter. To save the Tibetans would require the skills and endurance of the strongest of the climbers, Mallory, Somervell, Irvine and Norton himself, putting at risk the very men who had the best chances of reaching the summit of Everest.

Norton did not waver for an instant. 'The only thing that mattered,' he wrote, 'was to get the men down alive.' On his watch there would be no repeat of 1922, when a final effort by Mallory had resulted in seven Sherpas being swept to their deaths by an avalanche on the North Col.

Norton mounted what was certain to be a most precarious rescue operation. Movement up the col would be exceedingly slow and difficult. The danger of avalanche was acute; the snow conditions horrendous. Norton put the odds at 2/1 in favour of failure. Mallory in a letter home to Ruth thought 10/1 in failure's favour a better bet. On the eve of the attempt they gathered by candlelight in the mess tent and made plans for the morning. 'It was a gloomy little conference; we could not but recognise that to turn our backs once more on the mountain at this date might well mean the abandonment of all hope of success for the year.'

Through a truly heroic effort every one of the marooned men was saved, though it was a very close call. When Tom Longstaff read of the successful effort in the Indian papers, he famously exclaimed, 'Talk about pulling the whiskers of death – these folk crawled in through the chinks between the closed teeth!' It was later acknowledged that the transport officer Geoffrey Bruce was excluded from the rescue party because Norton, convinced that there was a good chance that all three of them would die, did not want to expose Bruce to the risk, knowing that his knowledge and skills would be needed to lead the survivors home to India.

There is no indication in the official camp diaries, in the private journals or letters of any of the climbers, or in any of the subsequent accounts and memoirs to suggest that any member of the expedition questioned Norton's decision to risk all to save the lives of the stranded Tibetans. At the same time, everyone understood what the rescue effort implied. As Edward Shebbeare reflected, 'This was the most daring and the most strenuous effort of the whole expedition and the resulting loss of condition by three of the strongest climbers may have cost us the mountain.'

For Norton, this was the ultimate test of leadership, and he never wavered for an instant. He was a man of action and deed, who found no time in a crisis for reflection or recriminations. Yet always he remained calm, in a manner that was both infectious and often salutary. If idleness drove Mallory to distraction, Norton's decision to rest and regroup as they moved up the mountain proved uncannily prescient. By bringing his men to altitude, and then leading them off the mountain for an extended period before returning to the heights, he inadvertently anticipated what in time would become standard mountaineering procedure for optimising acclimatisation at extreme elevations. And as Mallory paced and planned, Norton would slip away to enjoy the beauty of the moment and the natural wonder of the valleys that ran up against the flanks of Everest. An avid naturalist, Norton in his time in Tibet would collect over 400 botanical specimens, along with 120 varieties of butterflies and moths.

This ultimately is what made Teddy Norton and indeed all these early Everest climbers such compelling figures. They embodied traits of character we admire to this day, if only because they are so rarely encountered in a culture obsessed with self. These, after all, were men of discretion and decorum, a generation unprepared to litter the world with itself, unwilling to yield feelings to analysis, yet individuals so confident in their masculinity that they could speak of love between men without shame, collect butterflies in the dawn, paint watercolours in late morning, discuss Keats and Shelley over lunch and still be prepared to assault the flanks of Everest, or indeed the German front lines, by dusk. They were men the likes of which we will never know again. Their words and deeds both in peace and war will endure as a testament for the ages. And perhaps for us the most amazing thing of all is that these men were the generation of our grandfathers, and in the case of Hugh Norton, they were our fathers. This is something we should never forget and always honour.

WADE DAVIS

PREFACE

Some twelve years ago, my two elder brothers and I agreed that the life of our father, Teddy Norton, deserved to be recorded for a wider readership than just his own children and grandchildren. The lot fell on me to write the text, but in essence this is a family effort, though any errors or omissions are mine alone. Certainly their knowledge and memories of him were indispensable to the account I have put together, especially as he died when I was only eighteen. And they have patiently reviewed my drafts over many years, and corrected my mistakes and inaccuracies.

When eventually the first complete text was ready, it proved to be the wrong time to launch the book on the market, and it was put on the shelf for some years. But recently, the publication of two closely related volumes both dealing with the earliest expeditions to Mount Everest and my father's particular contributions to them (*The Fight for Everest 1924*, Vertebrate Publishing, and *Everest Revealed*, The History Press), together with the continuing interest of the reading public in these stories, encouraged me to take it off the shelf and try again. And this time I was fortunate to reach an agreement with Vertebrate Publishing to handle the publication.

Why my father's whole life, and not just his Himalayan mountaineering exploits, deserves to be remembered in this way I have tried to explain in the book, and I will not repeat it here. Readers will no doubt form their own conclusions. He knew how to live life to the full while keeping a firm grip on his own clear principles and values. It is a fact that many people who got to know him, at many points in his life, received a vivid and lasting impression of his charm, vitality and integrity. It is also true that his almost obsessive modesty meant that he left very few traces for the researcher. I have been heavily dependent on the memories of those who knew him to supplement the gaps in written records and in my own memory.

From the start it was clear to my brothers, Dick and Bill, and to me that his life did not fall neatly into a single category of readership, whether for military or mountaineering history. A proper account must blend these two themes, together with his highly individual range of interests in his leisure life, into a single coherent personality. This I have tried to achieve.

A brief explanation is necessary about spelling and other conventions that I have used. In the case of place names, including the names of mountains, I have very largely stuck to the spellings, and versions of names, that my father used and that were widely used in his time. Where this might baffle a modern reader, I have occasionally helped with a translation. In the case of units of measurement, I have again very largely adopted those current in my father's time and that he almost invariably used. This applies in particular to altitudes, which are given in feet – I apologise to present-day climbers who are undoubtedly much more familiar with the use of metres – and to distances over land, which are always quoted in miles, not kilometres. The text does include a number of words or phrases in Hindi or other Indian dialects that were much used in my father's vocabulary, but rather than append a glossary I have, where it seemed necessary and the context was unhelpful, offered a brief translation.

In addition, I must ask readers to bear in mind that the political map of the world was different in those days, and in particular that all references to 'India' imply the whole subcontinent that is now divided into India, Pakistan and Bangladesh.

HUGH NORTON
Manor Farm, Chew Stoke
August 2016

Teddy at Woolwich aged eighteen.

1

THE EARLY YEARS

Edward Norton, my father, played a prominent part in the British expeditions to Mount Everest in 1922 and 1924, the two earliest attempts to climb the world's highest mountain. Among devotees of Himalayan mountaineering history his name is well known, not only as the leader of the iconic expedition of 1924, in which George Mallory and Andrew Irvine lost their lives, but also as an outstanding performer in his own right at very high altitudes. His achievement in climbing without oxygen to within less than 1,000 feet of the summit in 1924 was unsurpassed for fifty-four years.

But his life was by no means dominated by mountaineering. He was a professional soldier, with a distinguished gallantry record in the First World War, who attained high rank in the British Army, and served in India on numerous occasions. Late in his career, he was appointed acting governor of Hong Kong, a highly unusual appointment for a serving soldier, in the critical year that preceded the Japanese occupation of the colony. He was a well-rounded man of many talents, with a much-admired gift for leadership, and a passion for observing and recording the natural world around him. He combined the avid curiosity of the natural polymath with a self-effacing modesty, qualities that were probably more admired in his generation than they are today. His life deserves a full account, so as to set his achievements on Mount Everest in their widest context.

BIRTH, PARENTAGE AND ANCESTRY

Edward Felix Norton, known to his intimates as 'Teddy' (as I shall call him from here on), was born on 21 February 1884 in Argentina, at San Isidro, a small town lying on the northern outskirts of Buenos Aires. He was the third child of forty-four-year-old Edward Norton, an investor in shipping, and Edith, the daughter of Sir Alfred Wills. His elder brother Jack and sister Amy were followed by three younger brothers and one younger sister (see family tree in appendices). The first three children of the seven were all born in Argentina, the last four in England. Their dates of birth spanned eighteen years, the gap that separated the eldest child, Jack, from the youngest, Dick.

This Edward Norton, Teddy's father, who would later be appointed a director of the Royal Mail Steam Packet Company, the Union-Castle Steamship Company, and Nelson Line, had started life as an entrepreneur. He set up a trading and shipping agency business in Hong Kong in his early twenties, and lived there for ten years.

During this time he made and lost two fortunes, the first of them at the gambling tables in Shanghai. The way he lost his first fortune was simple and instantaneous; he was mugged and left unconscious as he was stepping out of the casino with his winnings. The story goes that he was picked up, taken home and nursed back to health by a kindly Chinese lady. The second episode involved him in a long drawn-out lawsuit in London, trying to recover his losses from a former business partner. At this lawsuit, his case was represented by Alfred Wills, his future father-in-law, then an up-and-coming barrister. Edward may indeed have been of a litigious bent, as his wife's diary mentions his twice suing, in later years, an agency company he did business with. He won both cases. He seems to have been an active and enterprising member of Hong Kong society. In 1869, at the age of twenty-eight, he was a founder member of the Royal Hong Kong Yacht Club. Teddy spoke of Edward's 'keen love of small-boat sailing' after his death.

On leaving Hong Kong, Edward Norton returned to England and quickly became interested in trade between Liverpool and Argentina, in which he and two of his brothers all became involved. Argentina was at this time one of the leading economies of Latin America, and a magnet for many European – especially British – investors. His business and that of his younger brother Robert prospered, although his elder brother Herbert died, and was buried, in Argentina. By the time he became engaged to Edith Wills, his second wife, in 1876 – his first wife, by coincidence also named Edith, having died in Hong Kong – he was busy procuring land in a district of wild pampas 300 miles south-west of Buenos Aires, and turning it into a cattle ranch, an 'estancia'. This venture too prospered, and a successful ranch was established named Estancia La Ventura, which had, by 1883, a family residence comfortable enough for his wife and young children to join him there for a stay of several weeks.

Their home in Argentina, however, was a house named Quinta MacKinlay in San Isidro, in which they started their wedded life after being married by the British Consul in Rio de Janeiro on 11 October 1878. La Ventura was not Edward's only business interest in Argentina, nor his principal one. This was a shipping line that he co-founded with his brother, based in Buenos Aires, with the name of 'Norton Hermanos'. And again this venture was a success. It was still operating as late as the 1930s.

Edward's brother Robert also had a residence in Argentina, and it is clear that the Norton family's links with this country were strong. Edward's investment in farming land in Buenos Aires Province was by no means a unique venture for British expatriates with interests in Argentina, and when he and his family returned to England, he placed the management of his estancia in the hands of a resident British manager. In due course, his heirs were among the absentee landlords that became a popular political target during and after the presidency of Juan Perón in the 1950s. In the case of the Norton family this led to the expropriation of the property in 1959, and the cessation of their links with Argentina.

Edward Norton's father (Teddy's grandfather), also bearing the same name, had been a country solicitor in Norfolk during the first half of the nineteenth century. Before him the Nortons traced their ancestry back to a Norman family that supposedly came over with the Conqueror. Bearing the family name of Coigniers, subsequently anglicised to Conyers, they lived in a house that, to this day, bears the name Norton Conyers, near Ripon in North Yorkshire. In the fourteenth century, the heir to this property changed his name from Coigniers to Norton on marrying into a Yorkshire family of that name. The house remained the seat of the Nortons until the late sixteenth century, when the then head of the family, Richard Norton, a Roman Catholic, made the tactical error of joining the 'rising in the north', the unsuccessful rebellion of the earls of Westmorland and Northumberland against Queen Elizabeth I. For this he was attainted (that is, publicly disgraced), his lands in Yorkshire together with Norton Conyers were confiscated and conferred on one of the Queen's loyal supporters, whose descendants own the house to this day, and he went into exile where he died in 1585. One of his sons, Christopher Norton, having presumably taken a more prominent role, was attainted and executed after the rebellion was crushed.

The surviving offspring of Richard Norton relocated themselves further south. One branch, from which Edward Norton was descended, lived in East Anglia for some centuries, another in Yorkshire, where they were eventually ennobled in 1782 with the title Baron Grantley. On more tenuous evidence, the family claimed as its ancestor one of the regicides, Sir Gregory Norton, who signed the death warrant of King Charles I. There are records of a Colonel Dick Norton who fought on the side of parliament in the Civil War, and was a personal friend of Oliver Cromwell, but it is not clear whether he was a part of Edward Norton's ancestry.[1]

These were the landowning – and in later years professional – origins of the paternal family into which Teddy Norton was born. As to his mother's family, Edith Wills was the daughter by his first marriage of Alfred Wills (see family tree in appendices), born the son of a Birmingham solicitor in 1828, who made a prominent career in the law. After becoming a barrister in 1851, and a QC in 1872, he was appointed a judge, and received a knighthood in 1884, the year of Teddy Norton's birth. As a judge, the *Oxford Dictionary of National Biography* records, he was 'remembered by contemporaries for an austere integrity'. Most famously, if not notoriously, he presided at the trial of Oscar Wilde for gross indecency in 1895, and passed on him the sentence of two years' hard labour from which Wilde never really recovered. As well as serving on a number of public bodies, he edited and largely rewrote his father's reference work *Principles of Circumstantial Evidence*. Known as 'Wills on Circumstantial Evidence', it became a widely consulted textbook

---

1 This Dick Norton came from Southwick Park in Hampshire, where a descendant, also a Colonel Richard Norton, dying in 1732, made an 'extraordinary' will, which left his considerable fortune to 'the poor, hungry and thirsty, naked, and strangers, sick and wounded, and prisoners, to the end of the world'. Sadly however, as a contemporary record states, 'the will carried in it such evident marks of insanity, that it was soon after laid aside'.

of the legal profession for many years. He died near Southampton, of whose university he was in his later years chancellor, in August 1912.

More important for this story, however, was his equally notable distinction as a pioneering Victorian alpinist. He was a key member of that band of professional or leisured Englishmen who, in the mid nineteenth century, essentially invented the sport of modern mountaineering in the Alps. Their story, and Wills's, has been told many times. It suffices to say that at the start of his alpine climbing career he gained a high reputation from his ascent of the Wetterhorn in 1854 aged twenty-six, during his honeymoon, or more accurately from his lively account of it published in 1856, and that he joined with fellow enthusiasts to form the Alpine Club in 1857, the origin and forerunner of several alpine clubs elsewhere in Europe. He became its third president in 1864. Later in life, he was made an honorary member of the Club Alpin Français. Blessed with a naturally fluent and vivid prose style, he wrote a classic book about his Alpine exploits, *Wanderings among the High Alps* – in which the chapter containing his practical advice to mountain walkers is rather quaintly titled 'Hints to Pedestrians'.

Like many of his class and generation, he was a great deal more at home with the French language and with European literature and culture than his peers today. On his death in 1912, an obituary in the French periodical *La Montagne* noted that 'Monsieur Wills wrote and spoke our language with unusual elegance', and reflected that 'he was an admirable alpinist, very unlike those of today. Though capable of the most daring exploits, he despised gymnastic feats performed for their own sake, and asked for nothing from the mountains but their beauty'.

This is well illustrated by his account of a bivouac under the stars when benighted on an expedition among the high glaciers, published in an early collection of writings by Alpine Club members. It is a wonderful piece of evocative description, of which these extracts may give a flavour:

'It was a night I would not have missed, with all its inconveniences. The stars shone bright and clear out of the sky of jet; not a wreath of vapour could be seen; the solemn glacier far beneath us showed dimly through the gloom with a dead and spectral white, as if it had been some mighty giant lying in his shroud. The crags beyond it were sombre as a funeral pall, and, in the darkness, seemed to rise to such an enormous height, that the eye grew weary of wandering upwards, before their massive ebony was relieved by the liquid and transparent blackness of the sky, with its thousand glittering points of light. Not a sound broke the awful stillness of the scene, except the faint dashing of the distant torrent, which we had sought so unsuccessfully, and the crackling of the fire as R. heaped upon it fresh armfuls of bilberries and rhododendrons. Occasionally, by the fitful glare of the flames, I could see his form moving slowly and noiselessly about, now in bold relief against the ruddy light, now half hidden by the curling smoke, now illuminated by the blaze, as he passed round to the other side in search of fuel, quite unconscious of how much he was adding to the picturesqueness of the scene.'

Some hours later:

'And now we began to watch eagerly for the daybreak, for the sense of discomfort began rapidly to overpower every other feeling. You cannot – at least I never could – appreciate the picturesque, while the teeth are chattering with cold, and the inner man loudly proclaims its detestation of that which nature also abhors. That pale grey tint which steals over the eastern sky so imperceptibly that you hardly know it is there,

save for the sicklier glitter of the stars, how long before the
dawn it shows itself! How slowly does it ripen into light!
How it seems to intensify the power of frost, and to give a
sharper edge to the keenness of the wind! It was the most
protracted daybreak I ever remember. Again and again did
I turn my eyes resolutely away, that I might be sure, on looking
again, to see some signs of the advancing day. Again and
again was I doomed to disappointment, the only change
perceptible being that the sky looked colder and more pitiless
than before: the wind also was brisker and shrewder, and
wherever you posted yourself for a warm at the fire, in an
instant the breeze set in that direction, and you were
smothered and half-blinded by the smoke. But "come what
may, Time and the hour runs through the roughest day;"
and at last the grey faded into white, the white deepened into
yellow, the yellow kindled into a faint red blush, and the
highest peaks of the Aiguilles Dorées were once more tipped
with the welcome light of day. Our bivouac was ended, and,
having nothing to eat, we ate it, packed up our knapsacks,
and girt ourselves for the onward journey.'

We shall see that his grandson inherited his love of mountains, his
linguistic skills and his facility as a writer of good English.

In 1857, Wills and a small party including his favourite alpine guide
and constant companion on his climbs, Auguste Balmat, were descend-
ing from the summit of a modest peak north of Chamonix, Mont Buet,
into a valley unknown to him, the valley of Les Fonds, south of the
small village of Sixt. They came to a spot where a sloping grassy alp,
surrounded on all sides by conifer forests rising steeply to a girdle of
cliffs, levelled out into a small promontory like a ship's prow, before

plunging into the ravine formed by the flanking torrents. Wills turned to Balmat and exclaimed 'quel emplacement pour un chalet!' – what a site for a chalet!

He suited the action to the words. Within a few years, his mountain holiday home had been created on the very spot. Lucy, his first wife, who shared his enthusiasm for mountains, and was a talented artist – she illustrated *Wanderings* – designed the three-storey chalet-style house that was built on the promontory, but she died suddenly before it was completed. In his grief at her death, he dedicated to her his book describing the complicated story of its purchase and construction. After 'great deliberations', we are told by a contemporary account, it was decided to give the new house the name 'The Eagle's Nest' or 'Le Nid d'Aigle', but to generations of Wills's family it was simply known as 'The Chalet'. For decades, Alfred Wills and after him his daughter Edith returned to the Chalet summer after summer, usually with large and changing parties of relatives and friends, to relax, walk, picnic and, above all, to climb in the surrounding mountains. The Chalet remained in the family's possession for nearly a hundred years, and played an important part in the mountaineering education of many young people, among them Alfred's grandson Teddy.

Edith Wills, Teddy's mother and my grandmother, was Alfred's eldest child, born in 1855, one of two from his first marriage. A further five children followed from his second marriage. She found her life's fulfilment in making a home for her husband Edward Norton (who, despite his colourful early life, appears in the family records as a somewhat shadowy figure on the domestic scene) and their six surviving children including Teddy – a seventh died in infancy. But this should by no means be taken to suggest that she was submissive or uninteresting. She was a strong character and a true matriarch of her era, looked up to with affection and respect by her children and friends, not to mention an added degree of awe by her grandchildren. She had a firm sense of family tradition and the need to preserve the memory of their doings. She wrote, in clear flowing manuscript, the 'Record of the Edward Norton Family', known as the 'Family Record' for short, which she kept as a diary for forty-eight years from 1876, the year of her engagement at the age of twenty-one to Edward Norton, until 1924, the year after he died. The entries, including a few press cuttings, are factual and succinct, largely about her family, but with a few brief references to public events. They offer some insights into everyday life in Victorian and Edwardian times.

For example, being photographed was evidently a noteworthy family event. Every instance of family members, usually the children, being photographed – on one occasion by an 'itinerant photographer' – is recorded with the same solemnity as, and of course a lot more frequency than, vaccinations, having portraits painted or starting at a new school. Other everyday technological aids of life crept up on the Norton family slowly. On 9 July 1882, 'spoke through the telephone to the office for first time.' On 6 April 1899, Edith recorded that she 'bicycled beyond Fort Fareham!' – presumably a new skill. On 6 March 1903, 'Saw cinematograph of the Delhi Durbar'. On 2 June 1905, she was 'driven back home by W.A.W. in his motor – first motor drive'. And so on.

There are glimpses of the rather different climate of those days. In the winter of 1890/1891, on 13 December 'skating began and lasted till end of the year … January, frost continued, Fareham Creek all covered with ice on Jan 12. Skating lasted at least till Jan 19.' On 24 April 1908, 'Blizzard – over 6 inches of snow.' Occasionally, diary entries convey a more colourful picture. On 12 August 1901, while holidaying in Scotland, 'Drunken cook left, wheeled by Dad to boathouse, & rowed by Jack and Teddy to Strony. Sept. 9, wee John, the ghillie, very drunk and bit the cook!'

References to current affairs and public events are confined to very brief entries on royal deaths and funerals and successions to the throne, or put firmly into a family news context: 'Feb 16 1900, EFN [Teddy] taken ill with pneumonia … nursed … until he was fit to come home on March 1 – on which day Ladysmith was relieved.' The only extended entry on current affairs covers events in Buenos Aires in June 1880, with eight entries in the month and the word 'Revolution' added in the margin at a later date. Presumably, after that experience, it was difficult to get excited by the news in late Victorian and early Edwardian England.

A similar document was Edith's handwritten 'Short History of the Eagle's Nest', partly compiled from letters between her father and his second wife, a diary of the activities, year after year, of the summer visitors to the Chalet. The account begins in 1857 with the discovery of the site by Wills and Balmat, and was continued after Edith's death, in 1936, by other hands, finishing with an entry in 1958 in the handwriting of her eldest son Jack, recording the eventual sale of the Chalet to Charles Lucas. His entry concludes with the sad observation 'Sic transit …' [… "gloria mundi"] – so end all earthly glories'.

The Short History reflects, though it cannot fully convey, that after her father's death in 1912, and with the support, while he still lived, of her husband, Edith became the heart and soul of the annual gatherings at the Chalet. There she presided over, and provided the household management for, the large groups of relatives and friends. In addition, she was an ardent and active walker, and came to know the valley of Les Fonds and all its intricate corners as well as any of the family. She adored the Chalet, and it may well have been the very place she would have chosen to die, as she did, a few days after her eighty-first birthday, in July 1936. She was buried in Sixt, the village lying in the valley below Les Fonds. A suitable resting place for one who loved the valley and had spent so much of her time there.

CHILDHOOD AND SCHOOLING

These were the parents to whom Teddy Norton was born on 21 February 1884. His elder brother Jack was then four-and-a-half-years old, his sister Amy nearly two. All obtained Argentinian nationality by virtue of their birth in the country, in addition to British. In later life, Teddy used to say, perhaps jokingly, that he dared not go back to Argentina again until he was beyond military age, in case he was called up for military service. It is a fact that he did not revisit the country of his birth until well into his sixties.

The Family Record states that he weighed 'about' four-and-three-quarter pounds at birth. Whether or not this unusually light birth weight had anything to do with it, he did not enjoy robust health in his boyhood. As well as contracting chickenpox, mumps and measles, a common enough experience in those days no doubt, he also had a serious bout of diphtheria aged eleven, a potentially lethal affliction, during which 'gradually paralysis came on', and from which he did not fully recover for several months. Then, at the age of sixteen, he developed pneumonia while at school. These episodes of sickness make a strange contrast with the exceedingly fit and strong young man that he would shortly become.

The family left Argentina for good in November 1884, when he was barely nine months old, and set about finding a permanent home in England. He used to make, in later years, the curious but just plausible claim that his earliest memory in his life was of San Isidro. Back in England, the Nortons lodged initially at houses in Esher in Surrey and Botley in Hampshire, before moving in 1886 to Wallington Lodge in Fareham, near Portsmouth, where they lived for eight years. They then moved to Uplands, also in Fareham, and this became the family home for many years, until the mid 1920s. This family attachment to Fareham, which Teddy always regarded as his true home town, no doubt reflected his father's love of dinghy sailing, though there is little or no reference to this pursuit in the Family Record.

Teddy's early years and schooling were probably typical for a boy of his era and of his father's status in life. He attended a variety of village or local schools and received private tuition, with no evidence of academic distinction, and in May 1898 at the age of fourteen started boarding education at Charterhouse School, his brother Jack having attended Marlborough. He left Charterhouse after only two-and-a-half years; he thought it a poor school and was acutely unhappy there. Charterhouse did indeed go through a 'bad patch' at about this time, as a number of contemporary records reflect (and as did at least one other prominent public school, Winchester College) – possibly as a rebound from the overpowering influence of the great reforming headmaster Dr Haig Brown, who had retired in 1897. So his dislike of the school may have had some objective grounds. Much later, in a letter to his wife, he recalled those unhappy times, and how he had refused to unburden himself to his parents, but had bottled up his feelings and kept them to himself – an early sign of his lifelong reluctance to display strong emotions.

He did, however, while at Charterhouse, win a school prize for French and German. Together with his passing a national examination in French at the age of thirteen, this was an early example of the facility in languages that was a feature of his later life. He remarked to his son Bill that, once you had mastered a certain number of languages, learning new ones became progressively easier. When speaking French, though his accent was more clearly English than his wife's – whose French Swiss antecedents gave her a naturally good French accent – his fluency and grasp of the language was, so she declared, greater than hers.

Meanwhile at home, the Norton family had continued to expand. In December 1887 his second brother Arthur was born, only to die an infant death three months later on 20 March 1888, 'after being ill since Feb. 16', the Family Record states without elaboration. Then in January 1889 a further brother, Eric, followed. Always known in the family as Gen (short for 'the general', one of those mysterious family nicknames beloved by earlier generations), he, Jack and Teddy formed a close bond, particularly in their enjoyment of mountaineering, which lasted until Gen's untimely death in a skiing accident.

Next came Teddy's younger sister Hildegarde in 1893, always known as Gillie (with a hard 'G'), another of those nicknames, and finally in 1897 Richard Conyers (Dick) was born, the last of the Norton siblings, eighteen years younger than Jack and thirteen years younger than Teddy, though he was to die sooner than any of his older brothers.

STUDENT YEARS

What sort of a young man was Teddy growing up into? The record tells us little, and one can only speculate how much of his mature character was already formed. There is little suggestion that he was either studious or a lover of literature and the arts, though later he became well read and widely informed on many topics, and kept a fair-sized library of both fiction and non-fiction, with a particular love for Trollope and Kipling, of whose works he had complete collections. But unlike Jack, who went to Oxford and obtained a bachelor's degree in law, Teddy showed no interest in university studies, and instead set his heart on a career as a professional soldier. Where the interest in military matters came from is unclear. There was no soldiering in either his father's or his mother's family backgrounds. Perhaps his disenchantment with Charterhouse was so great that he leaped at any pretext for early departure.

The three older Norton brothers did, however, share a general love of adventure and challenges. An example of Jack's propensity for adventure, and perhaps also a clue to where authority lay in the family, occurs in the family record for the year 1900. Jack was then twenty, and eight months into his undergraduate studies at Oxford. Edith records that on February 12th she 'got letter from JHN asking her consent to his going to the war' (the Boer War), and that she 'went to make enquiries in London'. On March 1st, as we have seen, the relief of Ladysmith is recorded, and on March 19th she writes: 'Decided JHN should not go to the war'. And that, apparently, was that.

In June 1900, at the age of sixteen, Teddy sat the entrance examination for the Royal Military Academy at Woolwich, the training establishment for gunner and sapper officer cadets universally known as 'The Shop'. He obtained 116th place, but his family thought this was not good enough, so he sat it again in November, and passed in fifty-second place this time. He departed from Charterhouse, no doubt with great relief, and started at The Shop on 21 February 1901, his seventeenth birthday.

As with Charterhouse, not much is recorded of his time at Woolwich, except that he thoroughly enjoyed himself there, relishing the contrast to his school. He certainly looked back on it in later life with fondness. A formal portrait photo of him while at The Shop, wearing uniform and a pillbox cap, shows a good-looking, serious, clean-shaven face with regular features, but gives little clue to the personality behind them. Another, more informal, photo taken at the time by a fellow student shows him smoking a pipe with evident enjoyment and a sly grin. Starting at this early age, he was a constant pipe-smoker for the rest of his life, and his pipe and tobacco pouch accompanied him wherever he went. Also during his time at The Shop, he earned, for some now obscure reason, the nickname 'Reuben', by which he was known to many friends for decades.

In December 1902, just before Christmas, he passed out of The Shop, achieving twenty-fourth place in the final exams, and, as Edith succinctly records, 'got RFA' (the Royal Field Artillery). In March of the following year, after receiving his commission, he left home to join his first posting, the 71st Battery RFA, in the south of Ireland. He was nineteen years old, his student days were over, and his adult life and career were about to begin.

Edward Norton (Teddy's father, in white suit) on a salvage vessel in Hong Kong harbour, *c.*1860.

Teddy during a hunting trip (or 'on shikar') while stationed at Meerut.

2

SOLDIERING

IRELAND

In 1903, 71st Battery RFA was stationed in barracks at Clogheen, a small village some way from the southern Irish town of Clonmel, or as Teddy described it in a letter, '*in the wilds of County Tipperary, fifteen miles from anywhere.*' At this time, when resistance to the centuries-old British rule in Ireland was temporarily quiescent and the issue of Home Rule was not yet at fever pitch, units of the British Army were well distributed around the entire country. The purpose of stationing a battery of artillery in such a remote backwater is difficult to imagine, though it may be that, because of its very remoteness, there was an army training area close by.

Here he served for three and a half years. In a letter to his son Bill, many years later, he recalled his first Christmas at Clogheen, '*absolutely alone … with a whole battery on my hands*', getting tight on the compulsory intake of 'vile liquor', but added '*on the other hand, I had only to leave barracks 1/4 mile when I could climb straight up a 2,000 ft. heather-clad mountain with grand wild and very beautiful country all around*'.

This was the charmingly named Knockmealdown Mountains, just to the south of Clogheen. His taste for wild country and for mountains, already formed at the Chalet, was finding new outlets.

Indeed, he always looked back on his years in Ireland with affection. The landscape delighted him, and he was in a country legendary for its love affair with horses. The Family Record speaks of his coming second in a steeplechase a few months after his arrival, and certainly he hunted often. From his affection for Ireland came his fondness for Edith Somerville and Martin Ross's comic account of rural Irish society, *Some Experiences of an Irish R.M.*, one of his favourite pieces of light reading.

Of his military duties we know little, except that the amount of home leave granted in those days seems to have been, for a very junior officer, surprisingly generous. He visited his family in England in October 1903, for nearly a month in January and a month in November 1904, briefly in June 1905, for six weeks over the 1905–1906 Christmas and new year season, and for a fortnight in June 1906. Clearly the duties were not particularly onerous. In September 1906 he left 71st Battery and returned to England, on leave again, in preparation for the next phase of his career.

SEVEN YEARS AT MEERUT

On 7 November, having taken command of a draft in Cork (that is, an assemblage of troops from different units travelling together), he sailed for India to join the 3rd Battery RFA at Meerut, sixty-five miles north-east of Delhi. Meerut had been developed as a major military cantonment by the British shortly after it originally fell into British hands, and had been the home to a substantial number of British Army units since that time. It was also the location where the initial uprising of the Indian Mutiny had taken place.

Here he served, apart from some brief interludes, for seven years. Though he could not know it at the time, this was the first of six postings to India that were to be the centrepiece of his army career outside England – postings to Meerut, Lucknow, Bangalore and Quetta – three times (See map of India in appendices). He remained with the 3rd Battery for two years, and then the 64th Battery RFA for one year. In November 1910 he was transferred to R Battery, Royal Horse Artillery (RHA), and thus, as the jargon had it, 'got his jacket' – a reference to the colourful jacket worn by the RHA, even today, when in full dress. He would remain with the RHA, the elite wing of the gunners, in one unit or another, for a large part of the next ten years, including most of the First World War – the heart of his early military career.

At the start of this period, all guns of the field army were moved and deployed into action by teams of, typically, six horses. While mechanisation, and in particular tanks, started to appear in other parts of the army and also in the heavier gunner equipment during and after the First World War, the lighter guns, including those of the RHA, remained horse-drawn until, in the case of some units, nearly the start of the Second World War. The elite status of the RHA derived from its function of closely supporting the cavalry, which, being above all a mobile arm, demanded artillery support that was equally quick into and out of action. This then was the ethos of the battery Teddy joined in Meerut in 1910, and indeed of the other RHA batteries he served in afterwards.

During his first year at Meerut, he was detached from his battery for a few weeks to act as aide-de-camp (ADC) to the viceroy, Lord Minto, a man with robust views on the durability of the British Raj in India. It is recorded of Minto that, on receiving a dispatch from the secretary of state for India arguing that 'reforms may not save the Raj, but if they don't nothing else will', he replied 'when you say that if reforms do not save the Raj, nothing else will, I am afraid I must utterly disagree.

The Raj will not disappear in India as long as the British race remains what it is, because we shall fight for the Raj as hard as we have ever fought, if it comes to fighting, and we shall win as we have always won'. Events were to prove him wrong.

While at Meerut, Teddy Norton saw a lot of his battery commander in R Battery, Alexander Wardrop, a fierce, monocled 'fire-eater' of a soldier with a formidable reputation as a disciplinarian and high-flyer, whose views on the Raj may quite possibly have chimed with Lord Minto's. Teddy shared with Wardrop a passion for the sports of big-game shooting, pig-sticking and fishing. Pig-sticking, now almost a defunct sport consigned to history, was the pursuit and killing of wild boar, in areas where they were considered a pest and a menace to crop cultivation, by men on horseback armed with spears. The activity demanded considerable skill and good horsemanship, and could be dangerous to horses and sometimes to their riders, since the boars could be vicious and aggressive. Wardrop was a famous pig-sticker in his day, and wrote a manual of the sport, *Modern Pig-sticking*, partially illustrated by Teddy's vigorous line-and-wash drawings, whose accuracy was based on his own experiences. Wardrop was a winner of the Kadir Cup, the annual pig-sticking contest which officers from many units in India entered, and in which Teddy competed every year he was at Meerut. Although runner-up in one year, he did not succeed in winning the cup itself. He was, however, for much of the later part of his stint at Meerut, honorary secretary of the Meerut Tent Club, the prestigious pig-sticking club which among its other functions ran the Kadir Cup.

These two, with sundry other companions, spent many days and weeks of their leaves engaged in one or other of these sports. Teddy's sporting diaries record, vividly but with brevity, a catalogue of exploits. Rather surprisingly, given the jungle setting for many of the outings, bicycles feature prominently as a means of transport from place to place.

On 29 September 1910, '*Shooting, Asilpur 2 trees ... Bicycled Kithor. Pony to Asilpur. Camel back to K. Bicycled home'*. The diaries can seem monotonous, and sometimes rather too much a recital of killings, but the enjoyment he derived from the wild surroundings, the challenge of the sport, and simply from sighting wildlife is clear. Thus, on 20 May 1912, '*No sign of solitary bull, who has probably joined a herd. Saw swamp deer hinds one day, and, another, 2 sambhur stags in velvet. Met a bear on fire line at dawn one day*', and so forth.

Sometimes the wildlife nearly got its own back. An entry in April 1912 reads '*Met 3 bears. Missed. On closer acquaintance they coursed me some short way, about 4 yards off my heels. Jinking, I missed them again.*' He later described how, finding they were catching up with him, he had swung himself round a tree trunk and saw them cantering past just in front of him – bears being famously short-sighted.

Sometimes enormous patience was called for, and even then frustration might be the outcome. October 1913: '*16th – via top of hill to hide, 2 hours hard. There saw nice stag – 300 yds inside rakh. Watched him all day in hope of his leaving. 14 hours ... 18th – en route, saw stag in own nullah* [ravine]. *Spent day after him. Turned out a small one ... 20th – ditto. Fresh red bear tracks, into rakh. Out all day ... 23rd – ditto. To my joy stag and hind lay up for day on rakh boundary. Stalked from 9 till 3. En route lost Abdullah and wasted an hour looking for him. Grass shoes worn out – no grub. Stag moved down to water in my nullah as I got to within 150 yards or so of him. Followed – shot, missed. 15 hour day, 13 actual trekking. So after watching this stag for 7 days I at last got my chance – and missed! Better give up shooting!*'

For the first three years of his time at Meerut, Jack was also in India, though a long way away in Bangalore. After graduating with a law degree, he too had decided to enter the army, in his case the cavalry. He was gazetted to the 6th Dragoon Guards in October 1903, and sailed to

Bangalore in the following spring. That he took his career as a soldier less seriously than Teddy is suggested by the fact that he twice, in March and November 1906, refused promotion into other cavalry regiments, presumably preferring the lifestyle or the location of his original regiment. In December 1909 he resigned from the army and re-entered civilian life, back in England. He had been married in June of the same year – the two events were probably connected.

From this point on, his life was to be more sedentary, or rather more firmly rooted in England, than Teddy's, though he continued to be an active mountaineer and sportsman, and a keen horseman. He used to joke that he had been 'born in the saddle' in Argentina. As the years went by, he increasingly assumed from his father, as the eldest son in the family, responsibility for managing the affairs of the distant Argentine estancia. I remember him, much later in his life, as a relaxed, humorous, rather plump man, a contrast in appearance to my father's leaner and more athletic figure, and always with a twinkle in his eye and a joke on his lips.

Teddy spent his first Christmas in India staying with Jack. The following summer they were together again, big-game shooting – Jack shot a tiger. Intriguingly, they also planned a climbing expedition in the Himalaya in that year. Nanda Devi, which would have been a very ambitious expedition for two young men with only limited alpine experience, was considered as a target, and they reconnoitred the approaches to the mountain. But before actual mountaineering could begin, Teddy was recalled by telegram to his temporary appointment as ADC to the viceroy. The Himalaya did not feature again in either of the brothers' plans for a couple of decades.

As to Teddy's military career at Meerut, his activities as a sportsman featured more prominently in his memory than his professional life, but we may assume that his units were engaged in the continuous training and preparation for active service that characterises peacetime soldiering. Nor, in common with most of his contemporaries, did promotion come quickly. At the onset of the First World War, nearly twelve years after his initial commissioning, he still held the rank of lieutenant. But all that would change very shortly.

In January 1914, shortly before his thirtieth birthday, he arrived home on leave from India, and R Battery simultaneously left Meerut and was posted back to the gunner headquarters at Woolwich, where he joined it in March at the end of his leave. From March to July he was preparing to take his staff college examination. He did not enjoy the experience. His diary records '*working for Staff College March 1st to July 1st, a damnable time in a foul spot, Woolwich*'. Surprising perhaps, considering how much he had enjoyed his time at The Shop, but no doubt the words speak to his disillusionment with life in urban surroundings, and its contrast with the more artificial delights of the Indian jungles. The extended honeymoon of his life as a soldier was over. The harsher reality of active service was about to begin. The next ten years would expand his horizons and fill out his character in more ways than one.

During this summer, his mother's diary mentions that Teddy brought with him on a visit to Uplands his battery commander and sporting companion Wardrop. This was the first time that Wardrop ('W' as he became known) met the rest of the Norton family, and it sowed the seeds of romance with Teddy's older sister Amy. In due course she and W were married in 1920.

THE FIRST WORLD WAR

In Britain today, most people's knowledge of the First World War was until very recently probably confined to the fighting in the trenches, especially in the British sector, to a few household-name battles such as Ypres and the Somme, and to a vague awareness of the defeat at

Gallipoli in the Dardanelles. The many other fronts on which war was waged, involving British forces in most instances, are largely forgotten: the German invasion of Poland, Russia and Ukraine, the campaigns on the Austrian-Italian border, the complex struggles in the Balkan states, the British offensives against Germany's ally Turkey in Palestine and Mesopotamia, the British/German campaign in East Africa, and major naval battles in the Atlantic and Pacific oceans as well as in the North Sea. Any account of the war should at least make reference to this much wider context of fighting, in which the trench war on the Western Front was only one element, and not always the most critical one, either in military or political terms.

The account in this chapter will however follow the more limited scope we started with, since Teddy's First World War experience was entirely in France and Belgium, and his brother Dick's in Gallipoli and France. Both his other two brothers, Jack and Gen, also saw service in north-west Europe, though for briefer periods. In Gen's case, he was captured in Belgium and interned in Holland for the duration of the war. Nor will the fighting in the French sector feature, though the French-German conflict was titanic, involved several notable battles, and, numbered in casualties, was at least on a par with the British sector. The British sector was, in fact, a slight misnomer, as the declaration of war in August 1914 was made on behalf of the British Empire, and technically the big dominions had an obligation to take part. The Australians and New Zealanders fulfilled this expectation mainly with their large contribution to the Gallipoli campaign, but Canada sent a substantial army, and South Africa a smaller force, to fight alongside the British on the Western Front (as the battlefields of Belgium and France were known), and units of the Indian Army as well were sent to France and to Mesopotamia.

The character of the war on the Western Front is well known. After some initial skirmishes which, together with the manoeuvrings in the spring and summer of 1918, were the only instances of true mobile warfare, both sides dug and occupied elaborate trench systems which they used not so much defensively as in order to launch offensives; attacks which were often futile and disastrously expensive in lives. Sometimes one front or another was pushed back a short distance, and new lines of trenches were established. But in truth the outcome of nearly all these attacks was neither victory nor defeat but stalemate. In between these eruptions, identified as named battles but often lasting months rather than days or weeks, the trenches subsided into relative torpor, until the next military initiative was launched by one side or the other.

The British sector lay, for the most part, on the left flank of the Allied line, and thus in the early months British units were fighting as often in Belgium as in France. This was logical, since the German occupation of neutral Belgium was the technical reason for the British declaration of war – Britain being a guarantor of Belgium's neutrality. However, once the mobile phase of the war was over, only a very small area of Belgium, between the sea and just south of Ypres, lay behind the British front line. Only the first battle of Ypres and the battle of Mons belonged to this mobile phase, and in both the British were forced to retreat, and suffered heavy casualties.

Let us return to Teddy's war. In mid-August, following the outbreak of the Great War, he arrived in France, bringing with him the 3rd Brigade RHA's ammunition column which he had collected from Dublin. So began four and a half years of continuous service in France and Belgium, spanning the full duration of the war and a further six months after the armistice. Periods of home leave were few, according to the Family Record. A year and three quarters were spent in staff appointments, but for the rest of the time he was on regimental duty. He took part in a number of the best-known First World War battles, including Ypres, Arras and Cambrai.[1] Although the accounts of the fighting in this war usually focus on the hardships and horrors of life in the trenches, gunner records make it clear that the artillery in battle were at times closely involved in the thick of the fighting, and Teddy was on at least one occasion, in 1918, engaged in direct combat confrontation with German infantry. There was a huge contrast between this phase of his life and the preceding seven years in India.

In September 1914, just after arriving in France, he joined D Battery RHA as a section commander. In October and November the battery took part in intensive fighting in France, at Caëstre, and Belgium, near Messines (south of Ypres – he fought in the first battle of Ypres), and he was promoted to captain during this time. Although the official records of gallantry awards do not specify the exact date and time they were earned, it seems likely that this was the spell of fighting during which he was mentioned in dispatches, the first of three such mentions in the war. A mention in dispatches was the lowest ranked of the gallantry awards made during the First World War, given to individuals whose contribution during action merited a mention by name in official dispatches. Shortly after this, though again the lack of recorded citations means we have no details, he was awarded the Military Cross (MC), a newly instituted award for 'gallantry or meritorious service' first introduced in December 1914, ranking next up from a mention in dispatches. Both awards were gazetted in February of the following year, and his MC was one of the earliest awards of this medal.[2]

In January 1915, he was detached from D Battery and posted to the ammunition column of 6th Division near Armentières, across the French

---

[1] There were in fact three 'battles of Ypres', one each in 1914, 1915 and 1917.

[2] The battery's war diary also mentions that it was 'inspected by HM the King at the Vieux Berquin – Bailleul road in December'.

border to the south of Ypres, and then in March across to the 53rd Battery RFA, in the same district initially, then at Ypres itself. This tour of duty too was short-lived, but, as the months of April and May coincided with the second battle of Ypres, it may have been the scene of his second mention in dispatches, although that was not gazetted until the following year. A career change – a staff appointment as opposed to a line appointment – then took place in June 1915. He was promoted to brevet major (signifying a promotion with accelerated seniority, a mark of a high-flyer) and posted as brigade major RA (Royal Artillery), the most senior artillery staff officer appointment, to the 1st Canadian Divisional Artillery. Confirmation as substantive major followed in September 1916.

The Canadian Army contingent, which had been mobilised very rapidly in August 1914 and which, after crossing the Atlantic and under-going training in England, joined the British sector in March 1915, fought with distinction throughout the war. They had been in action at Ypres in 1915 before Teddy joined them, they were then in action again through a large part of the Battle of the Somme which lasted from July to November 1916, and again at the Battle of Arras in 1917, during which they carried out their most celebrated attack, capturing – over five days' fighting in April – a key German position at Vimy Ridge, a high point commanding excellent views over the flat Flanders plain. So successful were the Canadian front-line forces in combat that they came to be regarded as the 'storm troops of the British Army'.

The Battle of the Somme had been originally conceived as a joint British-French offensive designed to relieve the intense German pres-sure on the French position at Verdun, well to the south, though thanks to delays in launching it, the conflict at Verdun had in fact come to an end before the Somme offensive began. The Somme was characterised by very high casualties on both sides and by the appalling mud, which slowed down all troop advances to a miserable pace; perhaps only the third battle of Ypres, in 1917, rivalled it for the horrors of the mud.[3] It was significant in one other respect – primitive British tanks went into action for the first time, though they too fell victim to the muddy conditions and made little impact. Earlier in the battle horse-mounted cavalry had been in action, to no greater effect than the tanks.

Teddy now stayed attached to the Canadian Army in staff appointments for over a year and a half, initially as described, then from November 1915 until February 1917 as staff officer Royal Artillery to the Commander Corps Royal Artillery (CCRA) in the Canadian Corps headquarters. Few details survive of his service with the Canadians, though we know that the Corps headquarters moved more than once during this time, including several months on the Somme, where it was located through the summer of 1916.

We also know that he left the Canadian HQ at his own request, having become disenchanted with the Canadian CCRA, who he considered was ignorant of artillery matters and 'very touchy'. This was not the only time he would fall out with a superior officer of whom he had a low opinion. Notwithstanding this brush, he received, after the end of the war, a formal letter of thanks from the Canadian prime minister for his services to the Canadian forces – a document of its time, redolent with the ponderous style of officialdom.

> 'I desire, on behalf of the Canadian Government, to express their appreciation of the services rendered by you during the period of your attachment to the Canadian Forces in the Field in the Great War and to tender to you their thanks … The recent

---

3 It is related that the chief of staff of General Haig, the British commander-in-chief, visiting the fighting zone for the first time, burst into tears when his car ran into the mud, and cried 'Good God, did we really send men to fight in that?' His companion replied 'It's worse further up'.

intimate association in arms of officers of the Regular Army
with Canadian troops, all serving in the same formation, can
be productive of nothing but good and will tend to the further
co-operation of the two forces in peace, as well as in war. In a
larger sense, too, such a happy association cannot but conduce
to the still closer unity of the empire. Wishing you every
success in the future.'

In February 1917, when his attachment to the Canadian Corps came to
an end, he was posted back to D Battery RHA to take command of it,
an appointment that lasted until December 1920.

In the days before batteries were tightly combined into artillery
regiments, the battery, especially in the RHA, tended to be the main
independent fighting unit of the artillery, and the command of a
battery the first independent command that an officer could enjoy.
In Teddy's case, it was a turning point in his military career, coming at
the age of thirty-three and in the middle of a highly active phase of the
fighting, which would give him opportunities to distinguish himself.
It also brought him back into close contact with the rank and file
soldiery, which was the aspect of soldiering that he enjoyed most. So
much so that, later in his career, he reacted to a friend's congratulations
on a promotion with the words '*I'm not all that pleased, as it means I
shall never serve really close to ordinary soldiers again.*'

Immediately after he took over command, the battery moved to
Arras, and was in action in the battle of Arras, in bad weather and
deep snow, in mid-April. Further intense episodes of artillery warfare
followed in the remaining months of 1917. Late on in the year, in
November, at the tail end of the bloody and inconclusive third battle of
Ypres, a short action was fought at Cambrai, forty-five miles further to
the south and – a vital difference – over a terrain of dry, hard ground

much more suitable for the deployment of tanks, whose effectiveness had, with better design, improved considerably since 1916. D Battery was in action in support of the tanks.

Initially the attack was a marked success, compared to the disastrous adventures at Ypres and the Somme that had preceded it. General Sir Martin Farndale's *History of the Royal Regiment of Artillery, Western Front, 1914–18*, describing the first morning of the Battle of Cambrai, 20 November 1917, gives a vivid idea of how the guns performed on a successful day.

'[Before dawn there were] bursts of German artillery fire – was all lost? Tension gripped everyone. But the shells fell harmlessly behind the British; it was no more than the early morning hate, and by 0600 all was quiet again. But the tension was still there; after all, the operation order had warned everyone that the barrage would not be as accurate as they had been used to. The tension was great, too, at the guns. 10,000 gunners were poised, gun position officers looking at their watches as time crept slowly on and on to the inevitable zero hour. Then it came, a mighty roar heralding the battle; the battle of Cambrai was on. Major E.F. Norton, commanding D Battery RHA wrote "the batteries were literally flank to flank in two long lines as far as the eye could see, the rear tier firing over the front tier at 200–300 yards distance. The synchronisation was excellent and it was a most impressive sight to see the hillsides burst into a perfect sheet of flame." As the assaulting troops rose to their feet, the shells poured down in front of them with an accuracy that was unbelievable, hearts burst with relief, the pessimists were confounded, all was well, the guns – thank God, the guns – had performed the miracle and victory was certain. The Germans were stunned and dismayed, surprise was complete. Before the British tanks appeared, the enemy front trenches were overcome and when they did appear, the enemy panic was complete. Nothing could resist this powerful combination of guns, infantry and tanks.'

Farndale continues:

'But in this mighty hour of triumph, all was not quite right. The fortunes of war are fickle, the opportunities fleeting, and, unless commanders are well forward and able to make quick decisions, mighty opportunities are lost. At Cambrai, the British commanders were not well forward ... the fortunes of war did indeed change.'

His comment exemplifies the widely held opinion that, through most of the war, the many British generals – there were certainly exceptions – seldom visited the front lines or familiarised themselves with conditions there, but remained in their HQs behind the lines. The often repeated description of the British Army as 'lions led by donkeys' was for a long time attributed to a conversation between the German generals Ludendorff and Hindenburg, though its origins are in fact at least as early as the Crimean War.

After the stalemate at Cambrai that resulted from this shortcoming, desultory fighting continued through the winter. D Battery was shifted from place to place on the front, and by February 1918 was at Caulaincourt, considerably further south than its locations in earlier fighting, and indeed acting, it appears, in support of French as well as British Army units. Even in the thick of war, time was found for relaxation and sport. On 23 February, Teddy won a race at a point-to-point organised by the

Cavalry Corps. And since November 1916, his youngest brother Dick had joined him on the Western Front.

Dick had been commissioned into the RFA in 1915 at the age of seventeen, and saw action in the disastrous military adventure at Gallipoli, where he took part in the operations at Suvla Bay for four months up to December 1915. At this point he was hospitalised suffering from jaundice, sunstroke and 'general debility', first in Alexandria and then in England at Netley. The treatment and convalescence lasted seven months until he was finally passed fit by medical boards. He was then sent to the Western Front in September 1916, and posted to E Battery RHA in November as a subaltern. E Battery was deployed next to D more than once over the ensuing months, and was flanking D at Caulaincourt in mid-March 1918, at which point both batteries went into action near Jussy.

Abruptly, on 21 March 1918, the great German offensive began which would so nearly put an end to Allied chances in the war, and would in July bring the Germans to within forty miles of Paris before the tide turned against them. In the short space of three days, Teddy lived through the hectic experience of a fighting retreat, and suffered family tragedy as well. On 22 March, D Battery was heavily engaged in holding up the German attack, which on this front 'outnumbered the defenders by five to one at least'. E Battery was alongside D on the same day, and the D Battery diary describes Dick Norton, who 'happened to be standing by at the time ... hopping with excitement and filled with envy', shortly before E Battery too went into action to stem the German advance. But then on the 23rd, Dick, at the age of twenty, was killed while in action with E Battery. He was buried nearby two days later, in territory that was soon after overrun by the German advance.

Teddy had little time to mourn his brother's death. On the 24th, D was again in the thick of the battle. The battery diary records:

'After some time … a mass of men appeared on the ridge east of Bethancourt. After careful study through glasses, the battery commander reported these as the enemy and gave orders to fire. Colonel Mellor, however, was very doubtful and by his orders "stop" was given. It was almost impossible to make sure that the grey uniforms were not those of the French … The result of this uncertainty was the loss of many precious minutes. Major Norton gave the order to fire two or three times, but was each time stopped by Colonel Mellor … Finally, the behaviour of the men settled the matter. Their advanced machine gunners could be seen rushing forward and establishing themselves in commanding posts … almost at once the ridge we were occupying was swept by machine gun fire … The guns were run by hand under a shower of machine gun bullets, for our flashes were evidently visible and the enemy's machine gunners concentrating on the guns … Sergeants Pilbeam and Woollard handled their guns with great dash and coolness. Guns were run up until just not visible from Bethancourt, but the more they were run up, the more the Germans descended the opposite slope and it was at once evident that the only chance of hitting them was to run the guns well over the crest. With the concentration of machine guns opposite, this would probably have precluded the teams being able to withdraw them … The Battery Commander, with Colonel Mellor's approval, now gave orders to limber up and retire, with a view to taking up a position from which the line occupied and partly dug by the 18th Divisional infantry could be covered, for the guns were now the nearest troops to the enemy. It was a most difficult situation in which to make the right decision.'

Farndale comments on this whole engagement:

> 'The guns had been fought to the last with great gallantry,
> often being the only way to hold up the enemy attacks while
> new positions were organised in the rear … In sheer courage
> by the gunners, those were indeed great days'.

Shortly after this in April, Teddy was awarded the Distinguished Service Order (DSO). The DSO was strictly speaking a high award for 'meritorious or distinguished service in war', rather than a gallantry award as such, but during the First World War it was in practice only awarded for services while in action. Indeed, it is likely that it was sometimes used when a full recommendation for the Victoria Cross (VC), the highest gallantry award, could not be justified or corroborated. The brief entry in the *London Gazette* in July 1918 reads:

> 'For conspicuous gallantry and devotion to duty. He has
> earned distinction on many occasions, and invariably handled
> his battery under heavy fire with great skill; on one occasion
> fighting a rear-guard action with remarkable ability and
> coolness.'

There can be little doubt that the last words refer to the action of 24 March.

A curious episode followed the battle. A diary entry in early April by his mother records, 'War Office telegram saying EFN killed – but this was a mistake as he is safe and well'. Once again the brevity of the entry leaves us wondering what exactly happened. The War Office error may have been a result of confusion between Teddy and his brother Dick, though their parents had already been notified of Dick's death before the telegram arrived. In any case it surely must have caused redoubled distress at Uplands until they verified that he was safe and well.

Before concluding this account of Teddy's wartime experiences, a small anecdote throws some light on his attitude to warfare. He once told his son of an occasion when he spotted a German soldier carelessly exposed to view on top of the trenches. He wondered whether to shoot him (with a rifle), which he could easily have done, but could not bring himself to do it. 'It would have been cold-blooded murder'.

The months between March and September 1918 began with the apparently inexorable advance of the German armies, substantially reinforced since developments on the Eastern Front had enabled them to redeploy troops from there, till by mid-July they had swallowed up a large segment of French territory and reached their nearest point to Paris. Then the penalties of overextending themselves began to tell, as they had for the Allies many times in the earlier years of the war. A combination of increased Allied fighting forces, including American troops and further British reinforcements, and new battle tactics (at last!) enabled the Allies to turn the tide and start to press back the exhausted German forces on all fronts. By early August the Germans had fallen back to defensive lines approximating to their furthest withdrawals during the years 1915–1917, and further retreats, coinciding with a period of frantic diplomatic and political manoeuvring, followed up to November, when the armistice was finally agreed. Even then, the German front line remained almost entirely on foreign soil.

D Battery remained active on the now rapidly shifting front from March right up to the day of the armistice, 11 November 1918, when they were near Mons. Teddy was, according to the Family Record, 'at the head of the state procession' into Mons shortly afterwards. The battery stayed in Belgium until the following April, and in December he was mentioned in dispatches for the third time. He continued to command the battery for another two years, from April to December 1919 at Colchester, and for the whole of 1920 at Lucknow – his second, much shorter spell with the British Army in India.

INTERLUDE AT CHANAK

In January 1921 he finally left the battery that he had commanded with distinction for four years, and for the next year was a student at the staff college at Camberley, the army's mid-career leadership and management training establishment, an essential precursor to reaching high rank. Thus, nearly seven years after first preparing for the staff college entrance examination, he had finally arrived there.

The ensuing period of time between December 1921, when he left staff college, and September 1924 included the two early British expeditions to climb Mount Everest, in which he participated from beginning to end, each one occupying six or seven months of 1922 and 1924 respectively. How he came to be selected for these expeditions, and the momentous events that happened on them, are dealt with in a later chapter. In spite of the fame that came to him from them, for a brief period almost as a national figure, and among the mountaineering fraternity for much longer, they can be seen to some degree as an interruption to his professional career. In a letter written to his fiancée in 1925, there is evidence – where he refers to the Everest expeditions as '*a funny little slice out of my life*' – that he thought of them in this light himself, not with any regret at all, since they represented the crowning glory of his enduring fascination with mountains, but as a sort of irrelevance to his main calling in life.

Between the 1922 and 1924 expeditions, he was posted for ten months to Turkey, from October 1922 to August 1923, as brigade major RA to the 28th Division. The division was stationed at Chanak (now Çanakkale), on the southern shores of the Dardanelles, close to the historic location of the city of Troy. The prolonged peace treaty negotiations with Germany following the armistice had not resulted in a peace settlement with Turkey, the opposing army in the Gallipoli campaign. This peace settlement only came after the end of the Chanak affair. In the aftermath of the First World War, an outbreak of hostilities between Turkey and Greece on the Anatolian mainland had resulted in the rout of the Greek army, and the advance of Turkish forces up to the boundary of the neutral zone created around Chanak by a treaty of 1920. This boundary was manned by British troops, and in September 1922 Turkish and British troops were involved in an extremely tense confrontation that all but resulted in fighting. The British government under Lloyd George adopted a distinctly militaristic stance towards the Turkish advance, whereas the British public, and the canny General Harrington commanding the troops on the spot, were keen at all costs to avoid any further hostilities.

In this confusing situation, and in an atmosphere of great tension immediately after the confrontation of September 1922, Teddy was much involved in complex and delicate negotiations with the Turkish command in the area. He took the trouble to learn Turkish, an example of his facility with languages mentioned earlier. His experiences at Chanak, though brief, made a big impression on him, and he would recall them in a way that he never spoke about his time at Lucknow. He held the view that, next to the British, the German and Turkish armies were the finest fighting forces in the world, and spoke of the military qualities of both armies with great respect.

It was during his time in Chanak that his father died at home in Fareham, on 20 May 1923, having suffered ill health for a considerable period.

There is an odd footnote to his service in Turkey. He seems to have believed, at least at the start of this tour, that his career as a soldier was in the balance, and that redundancy was quite possibly in the offing. This is all the more surprising since it was shortly after the end of his time in Chanak that he received promotion to brevet lieutenant-colonel, more evidence of his fast-track promotion ladder. However, in a letter of November 1922 to Arthur Hinks of the Royal Geographical Society, one of the prime movers in the mounting of the early Everest expeditions, he wrote '*I am sorry that prospects of another expedition next year are not rosy, as I might find myself short of a job just about the right time … I may be 'axed', and shall then be able to disport myself at will*'. For a soldier with the career that actually lay before him, he was in a curiously diffident frame of mind about his prospects. He may have been wondering whether his recent eight-month absence from military duty on the 1922 Everest expedition had jeopardised his chances of continuing his army career. Whatever the reason for his unease, it was entirely unnecessary.

Officers from D Battery RHA at Mont Kemmel near Messines, November 1914.
Teddy Norton is on the left.

Teddy's self-portrait in pencil, aged *c*. thirty-seven.

3

A PEN PORTRAIT

It is time to recall briefly my father's physical appearance, and, more fully, his overall character, talents and interests.

At this period, in his prime, he was a slim, upright man who held himself well, very tall for his generation – nearly six feet four inches in height – and rather dashing in appearance. He had a forthright gaze and good eye contact. He kept himself fit by a tough regime of exercise, and during his climbing holidays at the Chalet was jokingly known to his family as 'the man of blood and iron'. He sported a trim moustache and, for the most part, dressed rather conventionally and in a slightly old-fashioned style. Indeed, although he was always well groomed and neatly turned out, he had absolutely no vanity about his appearance, and was neither a dandy nor a bohemian. His lifelong habit of pipe smoking I have mentioned before. He lost his hair at a rather early age, which he attributed to the soldier's constant wearing of headgear.

As to his overall character, I will start with his outstanding qualities as a leader. Numerous attempts have been made to pin down and describe this thing called leadership, yet in many ways it remains mysterious and intangible. Rather than try to argue that he was an outstanding leader, I will quote what a number of independent observers wrote or said about him over the years.

From a letter written by a subordinate officer from the battlefront to his parents in 1918:

> 'We have just had a bit of great news, and I want to be the first to pass it on to you. The major has been given the DSO. We are all simply delighted, as no one has ever deserved it more. He has been so perfectly splendid throughout this retreat, and we officers, and the men also, all know how much we owe to his coolness and resource at all times. It is such a very great pleasure to serve under him, that we all feel that we have the best battery commander in the British Army.'

From a private letter written to him in 1931:

> 'You probably don't realise what serving under a proper leader means to an ordinary person, who, like me, hasn't had very much of it in the army – because there aren't too many of you.'

From an officer serving under him in Madras District in India in 1938:

> 'If I may say so, you have impressed me as being the ideal general, and we do appreciate the interest you have taken in us, and especially the way in which you have taken up cudgels on our behalf.'

General Ambrose Pratt recorded a conversation he had in 1951 with

Field Marshal Montgomery, who had been (like the Duke of Wellington before him) disparaging about gunner officers:

> 'Surely that's unfair, sir. Many gunner brigadiers and generals would command formations well. Their leadership quality and human understanding is every bit as good as the same qualities in infantrymen.'

Monty:

> 'Give me an example'.

Pratt:

> 'General Norton. For years he has been an inspiration to generations of captains and subalterns in the regiment'

(i.e. the entire Royal Artillery). In similar vein, Jock Wedderburn-Maxwell, a soldier, commented in a published memoir:

> 'He was a man from whom a look or a word produced real friendship not to say loyalty, and was a *beau idéal* among gunners and in the world beyond.'

These quotes are from the military sphere, but lest we should think that the context of military discipline was essential, his talent for leadership was equally well shown, and perhaps reached its peak, on Mount Everest in 1924. This, despite the fact that he had been unexpectedly catapulted into the position of leader when the expedition was already under way. After his death, Howard Somervell, who partnered him on their high altitude climb that year, wrote to his widow:

> 'When he took over the leadership in 1924, he showed himself
> the ideal leader. He continually asked us all what our opinions
> were, and respected them, and then led in such a way that we
> all felt we had our hand in his, and were as it were yoked to
> him. Yet all the time he knew what was best and got us all to
> do it without any bossing or ordering – he pulling his side of
> the yoke while we pulled ours, and all in complete harmony.'

This eloquent account of leadership echoes the aphorism of the Chinese
sage Lao Tzu:

> 'When the best leader's work is done, his people say,
> we did it ourselves.'

Michael Ward, the Everest climber and member of the expedition that
first reached the summit in 1953, in his 2003 book reviewing the history
of Everest climbing, *Everest, a Thousand Years of Exploration*, describes
him as:

> 'Norton, probably the best of all Everest leaders'.

Alongside this gift of leadership lay a generous measure of dash, charm
and a sympathetic understanding of others, which impressed many who
met him. Photographs of him in his forties convey something of this
vigour and charisma. An episode in South India in 1938 illustrates his
sympathy with others' difficulties. A subordinate wrote thanking him,

> 'last but not least, for the manner in which you helped and

comforted all of us during the weeks of crisis and in the very
difficult decisions my wife and I were called upon to make ...
It is not too much to say that your help and sympathy on both
occasions were decisive and [we] ... regarded your spontaneous
advice on that black Sunday morning as an answer to prayer
... The crisis will always be associated in our minds with
Bangalore and of the friend to whom we could always turn.'

Eric Shipton, the distinguished mountaineer and explorer, was another acquaintance who was taken with this combination of dignity and charm, writing in the *Geographical Journal*:

'No one who met General Norton could fail to be impressed
by his personality, his quiet authority, his warm sympathy,
and above all his integrity. He inspired immediate respect
and affection.'

As for dash, he had throughout his life a love of adventure. His taste for the vigorous sports of hunting, pig-sticking and big-game shooting were indulged during his years in Meerut, as we have seen, and in the case of hunting through much of his life. He hugely enjoyed riding, and almost any sport involving horses. A charming sketch he made in Quetta in 1930 shows a tired horseman and mount plodding home at the end of a day's hunting, and conveys vividly his love of the moment – the cool of the evening and the pleasurable fatigue that follows a day's sport.

He certainly enjoyed some degree of risk-taking for its own sake. He was fond of quoting a couple of lines from Whyte-Melville on steeplechasing:

'No game was ever worth a rap, for a rational man to play, into
which no accident, no mishap, could possibly find its way'.

He chose his sports according to this philosophy. He once said in middle age, that, while not actually courting danger, he liked to '*get a good fright*' occasionally, as it helped '*keep my nerves in good order*'. An instance of this occurred when, at Aldershot in the 1930s, he wangled a seat on an aircraft performing a 'loop the loop' at an air show, '*in order to test my nerves*' – much to the discomfort of his wife. On the other hand, this tendency stopped well short of foolhardiness, as the prudence he showed on his high climb on Everest in 1924 amply demonstrates. He liked pushing himself to the limit, but never beyond it.

It was from this love of adventure that he applied for leave to join Ernest Shackleton's south polar expedition in 1914 – the expedition that culminated in Shackleton's astounding open boat voyage from Elephant Island to South Georgia. I am not clear what qualifications were required for such an application, but in any case, with the omens gathering for the start of the First World War, his military superiors refused to release him. My father much admired Shackleton's style of leadership, and may have consciously tried to emulate it. The description of Shackleton's huge relief when, on rejoining his crew on Elephant Island after a forced separation for the entire Antarctic winter, he learned that they had all survived, would have struck a chord with Teddy. When I was a boy, he used to quote Shackleton's open boat voyage, along with Captain Bligh's open boat voyage through the South Seas after the mutiny on the *Bounty*, as the two outstanding achievements of seamanship in the modern world. At the time I was unaware that he had himself tried to join that remarkable expedition.

Although in many ways far from the stereotype of a military man, he had some typical soldierly qualities. One was his neatness and love of order. With this went an insistence on punctuality. At home with his family, he liked mealtimes to follow a fixed schedule, which we were all expected to observe. His idea of punctuality, however, was just that – to be on time, but no more. He had no sympathy for those (including, it must be said, his elder brother Jack) who always turned up early, any more than for perpetual latecomers. An eyewitness described how he barely caught the boat train to Dover when leaving England to join the 1924 Everest expedition, arriving on the platform just at the last minute before its departure, and climbing on to the train after it started moving, but perfectly cool and deliberate.

He expected his sons to be well organised and self-disciplined, and could be a stern father. Displays of emotion, whether ebullience or dejection, were not encouraged. Nor was he himself demonstratively affectionate. He found other ways to express his affection for his sons. When we were little, he devoted time to creating coloured maps and illustrations of imaginary countries inhabited by our favourite toy animals, and inventing adventures for them. When we were older, he took great pains to teach us the activities that had given him so much pleasure in his life. He conducted himself on the same undemonstrative principles, seldom showed anger, was patient when it was needed, but liked directness, plain speaking, and honesty. He followed the simple precept that, if one gave one's word, one should keep it. 'His clear views of what's right and what's wrong' were commented on by an acquaintance writing to my mother in 1936.

He had a soldier's suspicion of politicians and politics, and was perhaps never completely at ease in urban, still less in pretentiously sophisticated, society. Yet he was always interested and well informed on world affairs and geopolitics. He was an enthusiast for maps, of which he always kept a good stock at home. In the days before television, listening with all his family to the 9 p.m. news on the radio was a fixed daily event.

At heart a countryman, he had an instinctive antipathy to most towns and cities. In 1940 he described Hong Kong, in an outburst of gloom in a letter to his wife, as '*a sort of foul oriental Bournemouth*'. When, later in life, he and she set off together by car to shop in Winchester, he would often take the earliest possible bus back to his country home while she was still shopping, if this avoided the prospect of having to kill time in a city. Conversely, his love of the countryside embraced the full spectrum, from the gently rounded chalk downs and fertile farmland of his Hampshire home, to wild and remote places at the other extreme.

He was the very opposite of a 'party animal', disliking equally the frivolous social round and the artificiality of formal occasions. His loathing for dancing was a family joke. His wife used to say that the only time he ever invited her on to the dance floor was with the terse phrase 'OK, let's muck in and get it over'. He was also more or less tone-deaf, and had no interest in listening to, still less performing, music of any description. It was said that the only song he ever sang before an audience was the Irish ballad 'The Mountains of Mourne'.

But he was in no way a solitary or a misanthrope. He enjoyed the company of like-minded people, and unbuttoned markedly in such gatherings. He had a talent for friendship, and kept many friends for decades. Alan Brooke, later Field Marshal Viscount Alanbrooke, and he were contemporaries at The Shop and at Meerut, and remained friends all his life. He similarly formed a lasting bond with Neville Gass, a gunner officer who served under him in the First World War – and in his subsequent career became chairman of the British Petroleum Company – who much later was chosen as godfather to Teddy's second son Bill. He had a close friendship with Sir Humphrey Trevelyan, a distinguished diplomat and Middle Eastern specialist whom he had first met in South India. Two long-lasting friendships from the mountaineering sphere were with Tom Longstaff, already a veteran Himalayan climber by the early twenties when Teddy was going to Everest, and with Howard Somervell, whose career as a medical missionary in India he followed with sympathetic interest over the years, on one occasion donating a new ward to Somervell's hospital but insisting, characteristically, that his name should not be identified as the donor. With his brothers Jack and Gen he had a close and warm relationship, founded on their shared interest in mountaineering and in challenges of all kinds, not to mention their similar world views.

As to his relationships with the opposite sex, up until this time in his life the family's collective memory is remarkably uninformative. His younger sister Gillie used to say, probably not entirely in jest, that he had 'never looked at another woman' in the years before he became engaged in 1925. Certainly there was no folklore about a series of girl-friends or a string of broken hearts, and his activities and preferences up to the age of forty were typical of a confirmed bachelor.

Brought up a Unitarian, in the sect to which his grandfather Wills belonged, he was certainly not a man of strong religious belief. With characteristic frankness, he made this clear to his believing fiancée during their engagement. He remained however a churchgoer in the Anglican Church. He regarded himself as 'rather Victorian', as he also told his fiancée, and indeed he did represent a number of Victorian virtues – self-reliance, stoicism, a strong belief in family values. In polit-ical and social views he was conservative, a traditionalist, and rather class-conscious, though no more so than was common in his generation. He was a loyal monarchist, and a believer in the strengths and virtues of the British Empire. Although today this belief is widely dismissed, he was an 'enlightened imperialist' who tried to live in his own life the values of justice, care and concern for the ruled that, in his view, the empire at its best stood for. His ideas on this subject were formed largely by his experiences in India, where he lived as a serving soldier over six separate postings between 1906 and 1942. He made good Indian friends and remained on cordial terms with them when back in England. In a letter of condolence to my mother following his death, his Indian Army friend General Prem Singh Gyani wrote:

'It is of course a great loss to you, but I too have lost in him, whom I had the privilege to look upon as a friend and guide … It was a most looked-forward to privilege to hear from him every year'.

His love of outdoor sports in his youth was gradually transformed, with the passage of years, into a keen fascination with nature and natural history, and also with weather, climate and astronomy. Starting in 1906, he kept for many years sporting diaries, written in a tidy hand and in pencil, and had them neatly bound in leather. Mainly consisting of factual details of his hunting and fishing experiences, they recorded in the margins a naturalist's observations on bird and plant life, and on weather and the passing of the seasons. Even when engaged in the sports that involved killing wildlife, he was always alert to the details of how wild animals and birds behave. Gradually these marginal commentaries, initially very sparse, begin to dominate. In his later years, when he was no longer active in the more demanding sports, he kept extensive natural history diaries, recording (for instance) in great detail his observations of migrant birds' earliest arrivals in England every spring.

He was especially a bird lover, and taught his sons to take an interest in ornithology from an early age. He emphasised the importance of song and voice recognition, so that we grew up birdwatching with our ears as much as with our eyes. But he was a keen amateur botanist and lepidopterist too. He liked to have in his library good works of reference on many topics. Consequently, in the era before the proliferation of field guides for the amateur naturalist, we were encouraged to consult the weighty volumes of Bentham and Hooker; the Reverend W.E. Johns; Dresser's *Manual of Palaearctic Birds;* and Witherby, Jourdain, Ticehurst and Tucker to help answer our questions about plants and birds.

The reverse side of this coin, his love of nature and the countryside, was his lack of aptitude, despite his profession as an artilleryman, for machinery and anything technological. He regarded this shortcoming with amusement, and certainly not with shame or as a serious disadvantage. He would quote a saying of his father's, '*I am just a mechanical fool!*' and clearly didn't mind if the same label was applied to himself.

As for the sports themselves, his long-lived love of hunting, fishing, shooting and, in his younger days, pig-sticking have been described. Of these, perhaps the one nearest to his heart was fishing, partly since his wife shared the passion for it, and they were often able to enjoy it together. But equally, any other sport involving horses (steeplechasing, showjumping) appealed to his keen interest in horses and his skill as a horseman, though flat racing was, for some reason, an emphatic exception to this.

Racket and ball games were also an outlet for his natural talent. He played tennis and squash all his active life, but also rackets and real tennis, both of which he thought excellent games, and pelota, a Spanish racket and ball game that he encountered on a visit to Argentina in his sixties, and promptly embarked on with enthusiasm. His love of mountains and mountaineering, the greatest sport of his life, is the subject of the next chapter.

His skill as a linguist has been mentioned. In spite of leaving school at sixteen, he had a fair grasp of Latin, and a wide range of Latin quotations at his command; perhaps typically of his generation, but certainly not of today's. He was convinced of the superiority of a classical education, which he urged on his younger sons in preference to mathematics, the sciences or modern languages. This belief in the classics, too, was a reflection of the late-nineteenth-century world, and its values and prejudices, in which he grew up.

His linguistic skills extended to his native language. He had the happy gift, like Alfred Wills but with more succinctness, of writing plain, fluent English that expressed his meaning clearly and simply. His dispatches to *The Times* when leading the 1924 Everest expedition, and his chapters in the official published account of the expedition, *The Fight for Everest 1924*, were much admired at the time as models of good English. They still read well. Here he is, for instance, giving a vivid account in *The Fight for Everest 1924* of the horrors of cooking and eating meals in a tent at the highest altitudes:

> '*I can honestly say that I know nothing – not even the exertion of steep climbing at these heights – which is so utterly exhausting or which calls for more determination than this hateful duty of high-altitude cooking. The process has to be repeated two or three times as, in addition to the preparation of the evening meal, a thermos flask or two must be filled with water for tomorrow's breakfast and the cooking pots must be washed up. Perhaps the most hateful part of the process is that some of the resultant mess must be eaten, and this itself is only achieved by willpower.*'

He had a notable talent as a draughtsman and painter. This talent was evident in his family as a whole. His mother was a landscape water-colourist of no mean standard in the mould of many Victorian ladies, his brother Jack was also a painter of landscape and still life, whose ability Teddy looked up to as greater than his own, and Jack's elder son Peter was a fine artist too, and taught painting professionally. A recently published collection of artists of the Alpine Club includes paintings by three members of his family – Jack, Teddy himself, and his second son Bill.

He was taught to paint in watercolours and in body colour (transparent watercolour supplemented by opaque Chinese white) by a family friend of his parents, by the name of Snape, whose work he admired. His landscapes, particularly of mountain scenery, flowed from his brush in every decade of his adult life, and at their best form delightful records of his travels, executed with a delicate but lively sense of colour. He would take small sketchbooks with him on many of his journeys, including both Everest expeditions, making on-the-spot sketches sometimes at great speed, and annotating them in pencil so that he could complete them at home.

But arguably he had a greater talent as a witty caricaturist in pencil, though he wrongly belittled it himself, regarding it as a trivial knack compared with the greater challenge of painting. His sharply observed pencil sketches poked affectionate fun at family members and friends on mountain holidays or at home. They are of such quality that he surely could have taken up the trade of cartoonist as a sideline. I remember two with special relish, the sketches he made of himself and his two brothers grotesquely reflected in a distorting mirror, on a day spent in a mountain hut waiting for the weather to clear; and a picture of himself and his three sons lined up in profile, each with their more unflattering characteristics emphasised, which he captioned 'What a good-looking family!'

Despite his aptitude as an artist, he was no great connoisseur of painting or of the visual arts generally. But an exception to this was his great liking for oriental rugs and carpets, of which over the years he made a small but well-judged collection. This was assembled mainly in the north-west frontiers of India, where itinerant rug salesmen, carrying their mostly Persian stock on the backs of bicycles, would knock on the doors of the more prosperous houses and lay out their wares on the veranda to be admired.

An anecdote he liked telling concerned his experiences after putting his rug collection into storage in London in 1938, before leaving for India. When eventually he was able to retrieve it from storage five years later, most if not all of the collection was badly damaged by insects. While trying to recover what he could from insurance, he took the rugs to a specialist Oriental rug trader and repairer in the East End of London, and enquired what could be done to mend them. The specialist, after an inspection, said 'these rugs are so damaged that I will not even quote you a price to repair them. It simply wouldn't be worth your while. However,' (after a pause) 'if you will give me that one, I will repair all the rest for you for free.' He pointed to an unusual, and badly worn, Persian rug whose origins my father had never been able to establish. Needless to say, he thanked the specialist very much and took the whole collection back home with him, and the valuable rug occupied pride of place from then on.

He had a dry sense of humour. In the last year of his life, he surprised his wife gazing fondly at a framed photo of their three sons standing on the summit of the Buet, relaxing from the climb, with the whole massif of Mont Blanc brilliantly sunlit in the background. 'Ah yes,' he said, 'I feel very proud of that picture ...' (a pause, while her heart swelled with pride too) '... it contains three pairs of my trousers!' He enjoyed recounting put-downs to himself or his status. While serving at the War Office in the 1920s, aged in his early forties, he would go for an early morning run in St James's Park, and recalled being followed by a mob of small boys yelling 'go it, grandpa!' In his brief stay in South Africa in 1942, he was travelling by bus to a lecture engagement, wearing a lieutenant-general's dress uniform, and was amused when an old lady, mistaking the uniform for the Salvation Army, pressed a coin into his hand murmuring 'for the cause'!

Allied, perhaps, to his verbal wit was his liking for puzzles. At home with his family in the evenings, *The Times* crossword puzzle was a daily ritual, with everyone encouraged to chip in. He would try his hand at compiling crosswords, too. He enjoyed verbal and mathematical puzzles, and had a few favourites of his own. He likewise enjoyed round-table games with his family in the evenings. For most of his life, his only card game was poker, which he played for many years, which appealed to his risk-taking instincts, and which he taught to his sons at a tender age. He would almost certainly have made a good, or very good, bridge player, a game which his wife enjoyed but which he never took up. Late in life he also discovered canasta, the card game craze of the 1940s and 1950s, which he took to enthusiastically.

His liking of a good read has been mentioned. His repertoire was not confined to nineteenth-century classics, but included contemporary novelists. He read, for instance, the works of C.S. Forester and Nevil Shute as they came out. Once he wrote to Forester politely challenging a navigational reference in one of his books, and was delighted to receive a friendly and contrite reply from the author.

My final and abiding memory of my father is of his modesty. Whatever his achievements in life, and some were considerable and, in the case of the Everest expeditions, outstanding, he was invariably modest and self-effacing about them, the very opposite of conceit or self-regard. When my mother urged him to write down his own account of his life, he would protest that it wasn't worth recording. Indeed, his reluctance ever to speak about himself and his experiences, however admirable a quality, had at least one serious drawback. I was eighteen when he died, and only realised much later – much too late – how seldom I had urged him to talk about all that he had seen and done. It has made it much harder to assemble this account of his life.

Some of a herd of
26 chamois seen thro'
telescope between Lion &
St Huberts Tower 18-VII-19. 7.45p.m.

Some of a group of twenty-six chamois, sketched by Teddy at the Chalet, 1919.

Teddy's sketch of a mountain path above the Chalet.

4

MOUNTAINEERING

A CLIMBER'S EDUCATION

Alfred Wills's Chalet in Haute-Savoie and its immediate surroundings formed a sort of Alpine paradise, whose influence on members of the Wills/Norton family it is hard to exaggerate. Year after year they were drawn back there by its powerful attraction, to relax, to take delight in remote and wild places, and for the many rock-climbing challenges in the Vallée des Fonds. The Chalet – and the tradition of climbing there, going back to Wills's choice of the spot for his mountain refuge – were the chief inspiration of Teddy's love of mountains and mountaineering. Even today, when the sky above Les Fonds is bisected by huge power cables strung between the ridges on either side, and one of France's *grandes randonnées* (or long-distance walkers' highways) passes just above the valley, it retains its secluded character, and is still inaccessible by paved road.

The mountain faces around the Chalet have a particular character, very different from the classic granite of the Chamonix area not many miles away. The rock is friable limestone. The climbing skills required are more those of balance and secure poise on steep, loose, unstable cliff faces and gullies, than of gymnastic feats on sharply delineated rock ridges. There could hardly have been a more suitable training ground to hone the skills of one who would, in due course, confront the north face of Mount Everest. Commenting on the insecure character of the climbs from his own experiences at the Chalet, Teddy's friend Tom Longstaff observed wryly, 'The Norton family are very careful climbers – when they've finished with their handholds they always replace them!'

In this unusual nursery for climbers, the three Norton brothers were taught to climb by their uncle, Jack Wills, whom they looked up to as a fine teacher. They would roam and clamber over the upper cliffs and faces, usually hunting the chamois which occurred in the mountains in much greater numbers in those days, or else simply attempting rock-climbing routes invented by the sons of Alfred Wills, or that they themselves had invented. The more formidable ones they returned to again and again until they succeeded. In their prime, they would compete in contests of fitness by racing from point to point among the mountains, like Alpine fell runners.

Ascending above the Chalet towards the south, the mountain walker, following paths used in former days for mule traffic, arrives at one of two cols that lie on the mountain ridge bounding Les Fonds on its southern side. On reaching either of these cols, a stunning prospect of Mont Blanc and the whole array of great Alpine peaks above Chamonix, eleven miles to the south, bursts on one's vision. This proximity meant that the Chalet could also serve as a point of departure for serious climbs in the Chamonix valley. The Norton brothers (or rather siblings, since their younger sister Gillie sometimes joined them), after walking over the passes from Les Fonds to the Chamonix area, engaged leading Chamonix guides to take them up classic snow, ice and rock routes. Here they were able to learn the skills of snow and ice climbing, which the lower mountains around the Chalet did not offer.

In 1921, for instance, they completed an energetic season of major routes on peaks surrounding the Chamonix valley. To traverse the Aiguille du Grépon, a rock classic of the Chamonix range, they engaged the great Josef Knubel, the erstwhile guide and companion of the celebrated mountaineer Geoffrey Winthrop Young. Teddy enjoyed telling an anecdote about Knubel on this occasion. After leaving the summit of the Grépon, climbers must abseil down a short but precipitous rock wall which was, in those days, only traversed on the descent, and considered virtually impossible to climb up. As they paused on a rock platform after the abseil, Knubel clapped his hand to his head with an exclamation of distress, 'My little yellow hat!' He had removed his trademark yellow woollen cap on the summit and forgotten to put it back on before the abseil. The brothers assumed that he would write it off to experience, but to their amazement the great man swarmed up the unclimbable vertical wall unroped without a moment's hesitation, retrieved his headgear and rejoined them in a trice, as though all in a normal day's work.

Between 1921 and 1928, Teddy, accompanied by various members of his family, climbed the Aiguilles du Peigne, du Chardonnet, des Grands Charmoz, du Grépon, du Dru (Grand and Petit), the Dent du Requin, and Mont Blanc. All of these were in the Chamonix area, all classic Alpine routes involving (with the exception of Mont Blanc) serious technical climbing, and all, in the widespread practice of that time, climbed with a guide. In the Zermatt/Arolla area he climbed the Rothorn, the Aiguilles Rouges d'Arolla, the Aiguilles de la Tsa (by the face) and du Lac Blanc, and the Petite Dent de Veisivi. There is no record of his climbing elsewhere in the Alps than in these two areas, and of course extensively in the Vallée des Fonds. Nor did he have experience of British rock climbs. And he does not appear to have climbed any of the classic Alpine routes prior to 1921. So, by the time of his selection to join the Mount Everest expedition of 1922, he was by no means an acknowledged mountaineer of the standard of (for instance) George Mallory, whose superior climbing skills and experience he always respected. The basis of his selection in 1922 was clearly something other than his reputation as a mountaineer alone.

MOUNT EVEREST

By 1920, Himalayan climbing was in its infancy, and a mere handful of climbers knew the region. Very few considerable Himalayan peaks had been climbed to the summit, though attempts had been made on a number. But aspirations to summit Mount Everest, recognised since the 1850s as the highest mountain in the world at slightly over 29,000 feet above sea level, had been afoot for decades among a number of explorers and adventurers.[1] Notable among them was Francis Younghusband, a soldier and official of the Indian Political Service, who had established a name for himself as the leader of an imperialistic military expedition to Lhasa, the capital of Tibet, in 1904, and had high-level trekking experience in the Himalaya. Since the governments of both Tibet and Nepal, on whose border Everest lies, were averse to allowing organised groups of foreigners of any description to enter their countries, a long drawn-out diplomatic campaign was an essential precursor to mounting an expedition. At this time Tibet seemed to be the less intransigent, and efforts were concentrated on getting permission for an approach to Everest from the north. These finally succeeded, and by early 1921 it became politically possible to mount an expedition to the world's highest mountain.

The British attitude to attempts on Everest was patriotic, in the sense that a successful conquest of the mountain would have been presented

[1] The height attributed to Everest in 1920 was 29,002 feet. Today, after all the intervening improvements in surveying technology, the widely accepted figure is 29,035 feet (8,850 metres).

to the world as a specifically British triumph. In January 1921, a Mount Everest Committee was set up in London to raise funds, to appoint the expedition leader and members, and generally to oversee the whole enterprise. The committee comprised equal numbers of representatives of the Royal Geographical Society (RGS) and the Alpine Club, the two bodies with the best claims to control the venture. The RGS represented the more exploratory aspects of the expedition, the Alpine Club the purely mountaineering aspects. Arthur Hinks of the RGS was the more vigorous of the two secretaries to the committee, and did a great deal of the groundwork required. He was energetic and wholly committed to the enterprise, but by nature rather opinionated and combative, and was prone to make enemies.

Sir Francis Younghusband, by then the president of the RGS, chaired the committee. This was appropriate enough. For a number of years he had personally promoted, and identified himself with, the whole idea of trying to climb Everest. The RGS seems to have dominated the proceedings in these early years. This is not surprising when one remembers that ignorance of the region around Everest was considerable. The early expeditions were expected to devote a lot of time to survey, map-making, geological and natural history investigations, in addition to actually trying to climb the mountain. Indeed, the ignorance extended to the basic facts of topography around Everest. For instance, Teddy's diary records that during the approach to Everest in 1922, when they reached the Pang La pass thirty-five miles north of the mountain, '*there was a tremendous argument as to whether the great rock peak facing us was Everest or not*' – this in spite of the presence of climbers who had already been to Everest in 1921. One of the committee's first decisions was to mount two expeditions, of which the first would concentrate on establishing the best approach route to Everest, and would not make a serious attempt to climb it.

It is easy to imagine how the announcement, in January 1921, of the intention to mount these expeditions must have excited Teddy Norton, given his attempt to enlist in Shackleton's polar expedition seven years earlier, his familiarity with northern India, and his love of mountains and remote places.

The reconnaissance expedition in the late summer of 1921, after exploring several possible approaches to Everest from the northern – that is the Tibetan – side, succeeded in identifying the only practical way of getting a party of climbers on to the north face, and thus within striking distance of the summit. This route on to the north face was via the North Col, a snow-and-ice-bound, 23,000-foot-high saddle at the foot of the face, which the expedition members reached, not without difficulty, and which was to be the gateway to the mountain used by all the expeditions of the 1920s and 1930s. The 1921 expedition also greatly improved the state of knowledge about the terrain and topography around Everest. It convinced the committee that the next expedition must make its attempt on the summit in the spring, before the monsoon struck the range, rather than during or after it.

Prominent among the members of the 1921 party was George Mallory, a thirty-five-year-old schoolmaster with a strong record as a climber on rock, snow and ice, and with an almost obsessive devotion to mountaineering challenges. A member of all three of the expeditions to Everest in the 1920s, his name was to become, and still is, closely associated with the mountain in the public mind.

How the membership of the 1921 and 1922 expeditions was selected is not entirely clear. The world of suitably qualified climbers or explorers, of any nationality, was a great deal smaller then than today, and members of the coterie were generally well known to one another. At the same time, Younghusband's very public announcement in January 1921 of the intention to send the first reconnaissance expedition, and in November

1921 of the first expedition aiming to actually climb Everest, attracted a large number of unsolicited written applications from several countries. This can hardly have been a surprise. They had to be sifted and, in most cases, replied to by the committee. The committee was taken aback to receive a number of applications from German nationals, and decided that they could not really be entertained in view of the recent hostilities. A note on the RGS's 1922 files draws attention to 'a number of applications from Germans who as ex-enemies were not considered suitable', and, more tersely, 'no reply to letters in German.' It was even more taken aback to receive, in 1923, an application from a woman to join the 1924 expedition, and she was politely but firmly discouraged.

THE 1922 EXPEDITION

The 1922 expedition, the first to make an attempt on the summit, was led by General Charles Bruce, a rumbustious, jovial soldier with explorer credentials and a good knowledge of northern India and its dialects. Always popular with the local people where he had served, he had wanted to lead the 1921 expedition, but had been prevented by the demands of his career at the time. The team under him notably contained George Mallory, and also an Australian, George Finch, who, apart from his strong record as a climber, was an expert in and enthusiast for the primitive oxygen equipment that was considered, in some quarters, an essential aid to climbing at very high altitudes. Scientific knowledge about the performance of the human frame under oxygen deprivation at over 23,000 feet was sparse. Some respected physiologists believed it would be impossible for men to spend the night at such altitudes and survive. They were soon proved wrong in 1922, but it is easy to forget how daunting the prospect of climbing to very high altitudes must have appeared at the time.

Opinion in the climbing fraternity over the propriety of using oxygen as an aid was deeply divided, with the majority of traditionalist

climbers at least dubious, if not positively disapproving. It did not help
that the equipment was technically unreliable. This controversy over
its use haunted both the expeditions in the 1920s, and it was scarcely
used at all during the four in the 1930s.

Two other 1922 expedition members would reappear in the 1924 party.
Howard Somervell, a surgeon from Cumberland, had wide climbing
experience and was powerfully built with great stamina. In 1923, he
moved to Travancore in South India as a medical missionary, and
devoted his life to this work. Geoffrey Bruce, a cousin of Charles Bruce,
was a young officer in the Gurkhas with absolutely no previous
climbing experience. He came to take charge of the transport arrangements, and ended up achieving an astonishing high altitude performance on Everest, the first mountain he had been on in his life. Both of
these two struck up a strong rapport with Teddy Norton.

It is difficult to trace the exact process by which Teddy became a member of the 1922 expedition. He was not yet, at the time, a member of
either the RGS or the Alpine Club – he was elected to the Alpine Club in
November 1922. He does not appear to have applied for a place himself.
There is some evidence that his uncle, one of the sons of Alfred Wills,
who was an Alpine Club member, vouched for him. It seems likely that
Tom Longstaff, a friend of the Norton brothers and already a veteran
Himalayan climber, supported his name strongly, and may have put
it forward in the first place. Probably his linguistic ability, and his
familiarity with some of the dialects used by the expedition's porters,
stood in his favour. In December 1921 the Everest Committee invited
him to go for a medical examination, and he was offered a firm place
on 29 December. When, in January 1922, the army granted him eight
months' leave, his going to Everest became a certainty. He took with
him on this expedition, and the subsequent one in 1924, his diary habit
from his earlier years as a sportsman. His Everest diaries, only recently

published, shared with those earlier ones the same dry, laconic and largely factual style, with occasional flashes of humour or emotion, the more striking because they are sparingly used.

These early expeditions were organised on the principle that putting two or three climbers on the summit of Everest required a huge underpinning of logistical and climbing support. The final summiteers would be, as it were, the tip of an enormous pyramid. Consequently the expeditions were very cumbersome, needing a large amount of administrative and logistical backup, and demanding of their leader management skills of a high order. General Bruce matched up well to this requirement.

All the expeditions in the 1920s and 1930s used the same general approach route to the mountain (see map in appendices). This involved starting from the railhead at Kalimpong in Sikkim, trekking north-east to cross the border into Tibet, and then west across the Tibetan plateau, and finally turning south to approach the mountain itself from a northerly direction. This journey took five to six weeks, and among other things served the purpose of allowing the climbers to acclimatise gradually to oxygen deprivation at higher altitudes. The route lay mainly across the high, arid and, in early spring, bitterly cold plateau. Teddy's 1922 diary contains vivid accounts of the horrors of the Tibetan wind. '*11.4.22 … By about 9 the wind (generally S.W.) is blowing bitterly keen off the snow mountains & increases in force until it begins to die down again at sunset, when night is generally still. This wind, as I said before, is like a toothache – one can't forget it.*' And again: '*19.4.22 … This wind beggars description – and ruins this country every p.m.*'

The approach march also gave scope for the observation and collection of flora and fauna. In the fashion of the times, these expeditions were regarded as rounded exercises in the exploration of an unfamiliar frontier territory, and not simply as projects to put a climber on the summit. Though the membership sometimes included a specialist naturalist, surveyor and so forth in addition to the climbers, multitasking was encouraged. To some extent, a spirit of amateurishness prevailed. Teddy in 1922 was asked to 'help with surveyor work', and to familiarise himself with a number of survey instruments and techniques which were unknown to him. He also undertook to make collections of flora, for Kew Gardens, and fauna, for the British Museum. The flowers and plants he collected and pressed. Birds and mammals he shot and skinned. Reptiles and fishes were preserved by pickling. There was butterfly collecting too. The preparation of specimens was time-consuming – '*Spent a hard p.m. skinning, and arranging flowers. Naturalist's job no sinecure*', comments his diary. In all this activity, he worked in close collaboration with the expedition's official doctor and naturalist (another dual role), Tom Longstaff.

Teddy kept systematic notes of his bird observations. As the climbers progressed up the mountain, they were followed by certain bird species in the hope of food scraps. Later, in 1924, one of his dispatches published in *The Times* recorded that '*I did meet a chough, at 27,000 feet. He only came to look at me, thinking me mad*' – the highest ever recorded bird sighting at ground level till then, and possibly since. Choughs were common on the lower slopes of Everest, and he had a liking for them, describing later how they '*used to walk over my legs while I was lying in the sun*' at Base Camp. All this appealed to his fascination with natural history. His diary entry of 24 April 1922 records, '*Wakefield found delightful gentian (like small acaulis) on absolutely bare sandstone scree, also saxifrage. I caught small Apollo-like butterfly – Longstaff a lizard. Descended through fine barren sandstone gorge (where G. Bruce, preceding us, saw herd of burhel* [wild sheep] *– easy shot for buck!) – the first game since Kampa. Saw Godslevski's meadow bunting. Charming camp on really green meadow at junction of 2 streams – away from village. Very peaceful and happy.*' 'Happy' is a word that crops up several times in the Everest diaries.

Of all the flora and fauna he met with, only one species failed to appeal – the leeches that abounded in the jungles of Sikkim at the start of the approach march, and about which he acquired quite a neurosis. One expedition member later told Teddy's wife that they were 'the only thing he had ever seen Norton afraid of'.

Amid a number of his records of shooting birds and mammals, it is curious to read (16 April 1922): *'In pm Longstaff and I took a stroll after birds: I shot a finch we can't identify with a catapult.'* A possible explanation for this schoolboyish choice of weapon lies in a letter written by the Mount Everest Committee in December 1921 to an applicant with strong naturalist qualifications: *'I think I may say however that there is not very much chance of sending a specialist naturalist next year, especially as the Tibetans objected to shooting this year, and that would very much hamper any further collecting.'*

Be that as it may, he brought back with him, and delivered to Kew and the British Museum in August 1922, large numbers of pressed flowers, boxes of bird skins and mammal skins, a book of his bird notes, a few pickled reptiles and fish, and 'a biscuit tin containing primula roots.' This last sounds like heroic improvisation, though Charles Darwin used to keep some of his plant collections in biscuit tins, presumably for their hermetic qualities, so perhaps it was not as amateurish as it may sound. Longstaff contributed an even larger collection.

On both the 1922 and 1924 expeditions, he also found time to fill his sketchbooks with watercolours of the mountain scenery, which include some of his best work of this genre, and, occasionally, colourful caricatures poking fun at his climbing companions. The diary entry for 13–14 April 1922 reads, *'gorgeous day – hot sun and hardly any wind. Yet sketching in blazing sun on 13th at 10 a.m. my water froze stiff on paper in a moment when I held paper in my own shadow. 19 to 24 degrees of frost each night.'* He was not the only artist of the party, as Howard Somervell painted extensively, and was in 1924 a sort of unofficial artist to the expedition. Almost unbelievably, Teddy records that, on their high-altitude climb in that year, he assumed, when Somervell lingered behind him on the descent, that he had sat down to '*sketch ... the effect of the sunset glow on the great panorama of peaks surrounding us.*' The idea of a Himalayan climber in those extreme conditions carrying sketching materials with him to record the view is startling, to say the least. In fact, as we shall see, Somervell's reason for staying back was something far more serious.

The 1922 expedition in due course arrived at the foot of Everest and set up Base Camp on 1 May. It was not a popular place. The 1922 Everest diary remarks that '*days were marked without exception by bitter blistering wind often starting at 8 a.m. & always continuing until 7 p.m. or so ... Everybody heartily detests this beastly spot.*' From Base Camp, the approach route to the mountain, established in 1921, involved advancing up a glaciated valley, the East Rongbuk Glacier, until blocked at its head by the North Col. The climb up to the North Col presented possibly the toughest technical challenge of the entire climbing route on this side of the mountain. From the North Col, at a height of 23,000 feet, the route lay up an indistinct ridge, known as the North Ridge, that formed the eastern boundary of the north face until, at a height of over 27,000 feet, it joined the main north-east ridge of Everest, leading directly to the summit. Beyond Base Camp, camps I, II and III lay at intervals along the East Rongbuk Glacier, and Camp IV was to be established just below the crest of the North Col. One higher camp was then envisaged before the north-east ridge was reached, and it was hoped that from that camp the final assault on the summit could be achieved in a day. This hope proved to be illusory.

Not far below and to the north of Base Camp, some sixteen miles from the summit of Everest, lay the Rongbuk Monastery, a major centre of Buddhist pilgrimage. Good relations with this monastery and its head lama were critical for all the pre-war expeditions, since the entire contingent of porters were Buddhists who regarded the lama with the utmost reverence. Any word of disapproval from him of the venture to climb Everest, which was regarded as a sacred mountain, would certainly have brought the expedition to an abrupt end. Fortunately the head lama in 1922, and 1924, Dzatrul Rinpoche, was a man of great presence, intelligence and wisdom, who quizzed the expedition closely as to their aims and motivation, and then pronounced his blessing and support for their attempt. Teddy admired him, and wrote in his diary of being '*much impressed by what we take to be a genuine saintly man*.'[2]

In the ensuing three weeks, the expedition succeeded in surmounting the North Col, and establishing Camp IV on it, and Camp V above it, the latter at a little over 25,000 feet. In due course, and with all the necessary preparation and backup, two summit parties set out on 20 May to attempt the final climb. The first, consisting of Mallory, Norton and Somervell, climbing without oxygen, reached just under 27,000 feet, while the second, Finch and Geoffrey Bruce, using oxygen, went to 27,300 feet. Though this was a great advance on altitudes attained by any previous Himalayan expedition, it was still a long way short of the top. They were climbing somewhere near the limit of their physical stamina, with clothing and equipment primitive and inadequate by today's standards. Henry Morshead, who should have been a member of the first of these high climbs, turned back suffering from severe frostbite, and later had a toe and some fingertips amputated. Mallory's account of the climb suggests that Morshead, a famously tough individual, may have been too cavalier about donning extra layers of warm clothing, and paid the price.

2 It has to be admitted that the head lama's declared support for the summit attempt was probably a little disingenuous, since he advised the porters, in a separate meeting, to try to ensure that the climbers did not actually reach, and defile, the sacred summit.

Teddy too was frostbitten, and in due course lost the tip of his right ear. His diary the night before the high climb records: '*Turned in early & spent a pretty bad night – sleeping 2 in a bag – I found my right ear had been frost bitten & I couldn't lie on that side – which didn't help much.*' This misfortune may have been connected with the loss of his rucksack, with all his spare warm clothes, earlier that day, when a careless rope movement by Mallory jerked it from his grasp, and sent it cartwheeling down a precipitous slope to the glacier thousands of feet below. Later on, he also suffered acute discomfort from a frostbitten foot, an experience that recurred in 1924, and for most of the return march across the Tibetan plateau was hobbling and unable to wear boots.

The expedition, thus far, had met mainly good weather conditions, which appeared to justify the choice of a pre-monsoon assault. But after the two summit attempts it was nearing the end of its campaign, and beginning to wind down. By a slightly curious decision of the leadership, the expedition was split. A number of the climbers, including Teddy, left Base Camp in early June. The plan was to spend some time in lower-altitude valleys to the east of the mountain to recover from their arduous exertions, before beginning the long trek back across the plateau. Indeed, the recuperative spell at lower altitudes was an integral part of the plans for these expeditions of the 1920s.

At this point, however, a decision was made by the remaining contingent to mount one further summit attempt. There had been a heavy snowfall, which, as it turned out, marked the beginning of the monsoon season. Trying to surmount the icefall below the North Col, the climbing party, consisting of Mallory, Somervell and Crawford with thirteen Sherpa porters, was avalanched, and seven of the Sherpas were swept over an ice cliff to their deaths. After that, as Teddy's diary puts it: '*Needless to say no further attempt was made – so Everest remains unconquered.*'

This horrible accident cast a pall over the expedition members as they set out for the return journey. In particular they deeply regretted that only Sherpas had perished in the accident. Somervell later wrote:

'I remember well the thought gnawing at my brain: "Only Sherpas and Bhotias killed – why, oh why could not one of us Britishers have shared their fate? I would gladly at that moment have been lying there dead in the snow, if only to give those fine chaps who had survived the feeling that we shared their loss, as we had indeed shared the risk."'

So ended the expedition, having achieved high altitude penetration short of the summit, but marred by the sad fatalities at the end.

Before leaving the story of 1922, it is worth mentioning the clothing worn by the climbers. Accounts of these early expeditions often emphasise its primitiveness. This can be exaggerated. The climbers did not go to high altitudes 'wearing Norfolk jackets', as has sometimes been stated. Their high-altitude clothing was the best available given the clothing technology of the time, there being as yet no mass market for severe-weather gear. During the approach march, they certainly wore old-fashioned jackets. Teddy's diary entry of April 27 1922 speaks of *'walking comfortably in shirt and tweed coat, sweater over shoulders,'* General Bruce jauntily described his 'very efficient mackintosh which covered everything' as being his (distinctly inadequate) protection from the cold for most of the approach march, and a photograph of Somervell at Base Camp shows him sporting a button-up cardigan.

But at high altitudes, the clothing appears rather less eccentric. There may be something quaint in the photographs of climbers wearing soft hats with hatbands, and puttees in lieu of climbing gaiters, at 27,000 feet, or sola topees on the Rongbuk Glacier, but we should remember that these were serious men wearing what they regarded as the best available kit for a serious challenge. Nailed rather than rubber-soled boots, and ice axes with very long shafts, were the leading-edge equipment of the day. Furthermore, a recent project that tried to recreate faithfully the clothing worn by these early expeditions concluded that in many respects, including warmth, it was not inferior to present-day clothing. In some respects it even appeared superior, for instance in its lighter weight and in allowing better flexibility of movement. On the question of whether the early Himalayan climbers were significantly handicapped by what they wore, the jury is still out.

THE 1924 EXPEDITION

For a number of reasons the successor to the 1922 expedition could not be mounted till 1924. Teddy had been in many ways a personal success with the 1922 expedition. In addition to performing well at high altitudes, his judgement had impressed some at least of the climbers. Hinks, who was no great admirer of Mallory, records that Mallory's judgement in climbing matters was thought 'inferior to Norton of whom everyone speaks very well'. He was accordingly a natural choice for the 1924 party, and in due course the army again granted him the necessary leave of absence for the expedition, unpaid after the first two months. By February 1924 he was forty years old, and although the significance of the ageing process at Himalayan altitudes was not yet well understood, there was a suspicion that he was not far from the 'too old to go very high' threshold. This did not, however, stop his older brother Jack from applying, in 1923 when he was forty-three years old, to join the 1924 expedition. His application was received with interest and passed the sifting process, so that he was shortlisted for the final decision on membership 'if his brother was not available, or even if he was'. However, he was finally passed over in favour of Teddy.

PLATE **1** A thirteen-pounder in action on the Western Front during the First World War.
PLATE **2** A horse-drawn battery moving between locations.

4

PLATE **3** Meerut, the Kadir Cup week, 1909. Teddy front row right, Wardrop back row centre, Alan Brooke back row right.

PLATE **4** Teddy's sketch – a sportsman's dream.

A is 3 Alpinists - Anglais I'll swear
Attracting all eyes in Argentière.

3 objects of interest
in Argentière 24-8-21

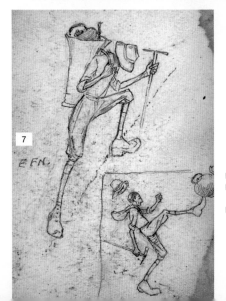

E.F.N.

PLATE **5** Chamois hunting in the Vallée des Fonds.
PLATE **6** Teddy imagines how the three brothers looked
as seen by mountain guides at Argentière.
PLATE **7** Teddy pokes fun at himself and the rigours
of carrying the picnic kettle.

WHAT A GOOD LOOKING FAMILY

PLATE **8** Teddy imagines a family group at Morestead (from left, Teddy, Hugh, Dick, Bill).

Everest
from Chogorong
15⁶/24

9

PLATE **9** Teddy's painting of Everest from Chogorong, looking due south, 1924.

PLATE **10** Josef Knubel in his little yellow cap, on the Aiguille du Grépon (page 63), 1921.
PLATE **11** Jack and Gen at the village of Lognan, above Argentière.

PLATE **12** Teddy resting during his high climb with Howard Somervell, 1924.
PLATE **13** Teddy's painting of Everest as seen from Pang La, looking south-south-west, 1924.
PLATE **14** Teddy goes on alone above 28,000 feet on 4 June; a photo by Somervell shortly before they separated.

14

15

PLATE **15** Teddy and Joyce on honeymoon in Corsica, January 1926.
PLATE **16** Teddy's painting of the Grandes Jorasses above Chamonix.
PLATE **17** Quetta, 1930. The end of a day's jackal hunting.

On voit bien
que c'est les
grandes Jorasses!
19 7/27

16

17

PLATE **18** Teddy (second from left) inspects air raid shelters in Hong Kong, prepared at his insistence against a Japanese attack.

PLATE **19** Teddy with members of Hong Kong's Executive Council, 1940.

PLATE **20** The Chalet in the 1990s.

21

22

PLATE **21** Sketches of birds seen at the Chalet, August 1919, with Teddy's on-the-spot notes on an unfamiliar
species to aid later identification.

PLATE **22** Distant chamois observed with a telescope.

23

Coronation + news of climbing Mt. Everest on June 2nd (May 29)

24

This completes a total of 9 weeks E n NE wind since end of Feb.

PLATE **23** Loch Urigall, Sutherland, 1952, painted during a light rain shower (of which some drops have left their mark on the paint surface).

PLATE **24** Pages from the June 1953 entry in Teddy Norton's natural history diaries. The left-hand page features a typically laconic comment on the news that Everest had finally been climbed by Sir John Hunt's expedition, which was released on the day of the Queen's coronation.

'6?   Since above no more rain: strong NE winds until 4th when it
        turned really hot at last - for 1st time for nearly 8 months.   No
        fire all yesterday & shed all my winter clothes.   JHN saw
        spotted flycatcher on about May 3rd.

9   Heard garden warbler in woods at West Lodge - Prolonged
        anti-cyclone into cold E winds continues

13   Wind went round to S.

14   Light rain in night. End of anticyclone & fortnights danger with
        continuous E. winds - no more rain in day.

15   Steady rain all night - Wood warblers singing near
        West Lodge gate.

21st   A good deal of rain in night after a few warm but
        unsettled days.

24   Great change in temperature - 78° at Monewden nearly 90° -
to
26?   London with v. high humidity. Extraordinary effect on
        vegetation. Growth of all sorts in a few days quite phenomenal

JUNE   Since above weather turned v. cold with strong NE wind + a
8?   lot of rain in midlands at Coronation time though hardly
        any here. - NE wind persists & we have had fires two or
        three nights - Phenomenal growth continues - only two
        nesting boxes occupied   Believe stone curlews
        are nesting in Churchlands (north)

10?   NE wind continues - cloudless skies - garden badly need rain.

29ᵗ Nightingales + White Throats at Longwood Warren
    Sparrow Hawk tower Gallops

30ᵗ Wind turned W. & glass falling. Since April 4ᵗ
    absolute drought + continuous NE wind very strong for
    the most part. The whole country is parched

MAY

2ⁿᵈ. Started to rain about 6 pm & rained intermittently all
    night – Hail early this morning.

8 Rained all day on 3ʳᵈ but mostly light – we could well do
    with a lot more – Since then only a few light showers
    Remains very cold

9 Our Copper beach remains quite leafless & all trees are
    very backward owing to lack of rain + a lot of ground
    frosts persisting up to 8ᵗ   Yesterday was warmest day
    to date though wind still cold. House martins in some numbers

12ᵗ Two perfect hot cloudless days with temp. up to 73° daily
    + quite warm nights + hardly a cloud in the sky – Copper
    beech burst into leaf – Ground very parched. Pigeons
    destroying vegetables. Tremendous run on bird bath.
    No more house martins since 9ᵗʰ ÷ Have been
    clearing up rockery + applying weed killer for last 3
    days – Chestnut in full flower

13 Temp. 76° y'day. – minimum 53° – House martin prospecting again

25

The 1924 expedition proved to be a more challenging affair than the 1922, largely because of much more adverse weather conditions. General Bruce again led the expedition, though his medical examiners were dubious about his fitness, detecting his doubtful heart condition, but apparently missing his recurrent malaria. One of them wrote enigmatically to the Mount Everest Committee's secretary, 'I am very interested to know if General Bruce is joining. I hope he is, but think he shouldn't!'

Bruce and the committee appointed Teddy as his second in command and climbing leader. Mallory, though unquestionably a very strong candidate for this double appointment, held back from offering to join the expedition until the membership was almost fully decided. When he did, and was of course accepted, Teddy immediately asked for his appointment to be offered to Mallory instead. As he later wrote to the French alpinist and writer Claire Engel, Mallory *was the only member with two years' experience of the mountain. He must have felt, therefore, that he was entitled to the position of second-in-command and leader of the climbing party to which I had already been appointed by Bruce. I in fact offered to stand down in his favour.* But Bruce declined to change his mind, so the appointment stood, after which Mallory, *backed me in the most generous and whole-hearted way … I think his conduct showed a singularly generous spirit.* And to Mallory's widow, after his death, he wrote, *Owing to his having joined the expedition so late I always felt that I had usurped the place he would otherwise have filled. I was always conscious of the inferiority of my qualifications to do so and guessed he might feel the same. Yet never once by word or deed or hint did he suggest such a thing. He simply played up to me and backed me up through thick and thin. In every detail of the mountain campaign we worked in together and his unfailing sound advice, his organising ability, his bottomless capacity for work and his determination to win were my prop and stay.*

Geoffrey Bruce and Howard Somervell were again members of the 1924 expedition. Among the newcomers to the climbing contingent was Noel Odell, a geologist whom Teddy described in a private letter as '*a very slow starter, physically and mentally, for he acclimatised very slowly ... The more credit to him that in the end he proved a complete winner. His performance in going twice to 27,000 feet and finishing up as fresh as paint is an astonishing one. He simply worked like a horse at all subsidiary jobs.*' He also had good mechanical aptitude, and in this he was matched by another newcomer, Andrew (Sandy) Irvine, at twenty-two much the youngest member of the party, not an experienced climber, but a very strong and likeable young man who had impressed as an explorer on a recent expedition to Spitsbergen.

Odell and Irvine worked tirelessly at maintaining or modifying the oxygen equipment, for, as the non-believers had predicted, there were considerable mechanical problems. Teddy himself was no enthusiast for the use of oxygen, though he was careful not to express his views too publicly. He wrote in his diary during the approach march, '*the apparatus is failing all along the line – thirty-three cylinders out of ninety have leaked – almost every instrument leaks at joint and tube – but for the mechanical genius of Odell and Irvine we should be hopelessly done*'; and in a private letter after the end of the expedition spoke of '*the b****y oxygen (which was mechanically a complete failure this year)*'. Of Irvine himself, he wrote '*Young Irvine was a champion in every way. Better mechanic even than Finch, a tremendous worker, strong goer with the guts of an Oxford blue. Personally I never had the chance of vetting his mountaineering capabilities.*'

George Finch, who undoubtedly had a very good claim to selection, was omitted by the committee. To many this seemed a bizarre decision. He had, however, alienated a number of the committee members in the aftermath of the 1922 expedition, by public lecturing activities allegedly in breach of an agreement with the committee, and was not going to be forgiven. The final member of the climbing team was John Hazard, the last man to be selected. He played a significant part in the high climbing in 1924, but was not particularly popular, gaining the reputation of being a solitary individualist rather than a team player. Teddy described him discreetly as one 'who works best on his own'.

The Sherpa, Bhotia and Tibetan porters hired by the expedition were generally admired by the climbers, and Teddy was no exception. His 1924 diary comments during the approach march, '*as often before I am lost in admiration of the servants, porters etc., who walk 18 miles in bitter weather, get into camp and work like beavers to get their sahibs fed, clothed and housed.*' In a letter to Younghusband he speaks of the climbers' comfortable nights in the high camps being '*the achievement of our fine porters … It is a curious psychological fact that here are men – on the spot – who could climb Everest without turning a hair. Yet the sahib – so physically inferior in this respect – has to come 1000s of miles to give them a lead – even to 27000 ft.*' He learned, or at least had a smattering of, four of the languages or dialects spoken by the porters, and found it on more than one occasion a vital skill in a tight spot.

The expedition left Kalimpong in Sikkim on 28 March to start the five-week trek across the Tibetan plateau. Partly thanks to the reunion of several members who knew each other from the 1922 expedition, it seems to have been a harmonious and high-spirited party. As an example, Teddy and several of the other members jumped from the slow-moving train from Siliguri to Darjeeling at the start of a loop in the railway line, and raced each other up the mountainside just in time to rejoin the train, still in motion, at the upper end of the loop. A few days later, his diary notes on 1 April 1924 that '*Geoff* [Bruce, who had gone ahead to find a new campsite] *left us half a bottle of whisky, which turned out to be tea. We failed to connect this with April 1st.*'

Before long, however, sickness began to take its toll on some of the party. Bentley Beetham, an experienced mountaineer of whom much had been expected, was afflicted by acute dysentery, which kept him out of contention for virtually the whole expedition. And General Bruce was struck down by a severe bout of malaria. While the rest of the party advanced across the plateau, he was detained under doctor's orders, and eventually pronounced unfit to proceed any further. Teddy's diary records on 13 April, '*In p.m. arrived the sad news that Genl has had to turn back from Tuna – for good, accompanied by Hingston* [the expedition doctor]. *So I now carry on*' – or, as we would say nowadays, 'take over'.

These five laconic words signalled the start of his leadership of the expedition, which was to prove more testing than he could have foreseen. One of his first acts was to appoint Mallory as his deputy and leader of the climbing party. These two became the lynchpin of the climbing strategy, which was thrashed out as they advanced towards the mountain. He afterwards described the initial strategy as '*largely the outcome of a friendly conflict of opinion, and finally a compromise between Mallory and me, though Mallory evolved it.*' He was punctilious in respecting his delegation of the climbing leadership to Mallory, to whom he left entirely the decision as to his own inclusion in the high altitude parties.

One element, though by no means the only one, in the strategy discussions was the choice of route to the summit from the final camp high up on the North Ridge. There were two options. One was to climb up to the North-East Ridge and then follow it all the way to the top. This would undoubtedly have been the natural choice for most climbers, were it not for one great drawback, a formidably steep rock feature blocking the ridge, known as the Second Step. The other option was to traverse across the face of the mountain parallel to the North-East ridge, avoiding the Second Step by passing below it, and eventually climb directly to the top up the 'summit pyramid'. Mallory, as a gifted rock climber with high-grade Welsh as well as Alpine experience, was naturally drawn to the knife-edged north-east ridge. Teddy, with his Chalet experience, more readily favoured the lower traverse, so similar in character to the terrain he knew well from his early climbing days. They discussed this choice repeatedly during the approach march, without either one persuading the other. No doubt this formed part of the 'friendly conflict of opinion'.

Among the duties Teddy took over from Bruce as expedition leader was the writing of regular dispatches on their progress to *The Times*, which had contracted with the committee for the exclusive right to publish them. In addition he wrote regular reports to the committee. The diary entry of 23 April reads, '*Later finished report to Mt Everest Committee & Times article and began a letter to General. One doesn't get much time to oneself these days!*' And, in a burst of self-disparagement, on 20 April, '*Spent p.m. writing Times article – fearful tripe – I only hope British public will like it.*'

Arthur Hinks, writing to him regularly, fussed about the commitment to produce a total of fifteen *Times* dispatches, and urged him to plan them so that the later dispatches would cover the climax of the ascent. Hinks, who had an impractical streak, failed to allow for the time his letters, all delivered by runner from Kalimpong, would take to reach their addressee, who commented tersely in his reply of 23 June, '*You again* [in Hinks's letter of 30 April] *refer to the telegrams, and suggest my getting in quite a number before the climbing. This letter reached me six weeks after the climbing began*' and, he might have added, nearly two weeks after they departed from Base Camp on the return journey. In spite of this misunderstanding, Hinks, whose letters convey his warm support to the acting leader, admired Teddy's descriptive prose, which he contrasted with Bruce's more flippant, throwaway style. In a later letter, he wrote that he intended to reprint most of *The Times* dispatches in the RGS's organ, the *Geographical Journal*, and this was duly done.

The expedition pitched Base Camp at the foot of Everest on 29 April, and from then on met considerably worse weather than in 1922. Twice during May they attempted to push forward to Camp IV on the North Col and from it gain access to the upper slopes of the mountain, and twice they were beaten back by violent weather with heavy snow-storms, on both occasions having to withdraw completely to Camp I or Base Camp to recuperate. Inevitably the fitness of the whole party deteriorated. After the first of these retreats, it was decided, in the light of the general state of lowered morale among the porters, to seek the blessing of the head lama of Rongbuk Monastery. The entire expedition accordingly trekked down to the monastery, where the lama duly blessed every member individually. He then delivered (in the words of Geoffrey Bruce's account) a

> 'short but impressive address, encouraging the men to persevere, and assuring them that he would personally pray for them ... His prayers and blessing put fresh heart into them, and on the return journey to Base Camp they were very nearly their cheery normal selves once more.'

The episode underlines the importance of the head lama to the expedition's chances of success.

The second of the retreats from the North Col posed a desperate challenge to the climbers. Four Sherpa porters were stranded at Camp IV after a heavy snowfall. The bad weather already threatened avalanches, and the porters were seriously short of food. So in spite of all the climbers being weakened by poor health or exhaustion or both, they were obliged to mount a rescue attempt from Camp III at the foot of the icefall. The memory of the tragic accident at this very place in 1922 hung over them. It was decided that Teddy, with Mallory and Somervell, would go up to the col and bring the marooned porters down safely. His diary records, '*I slept little thinking of most unpleasant job ahead of us (Mallory and I afterwards agreed that we both put our chances of being avalanched at about 2 to 1 on) & of horrible situation if we failed to rescue these men – chances of some being too frostbitten to come down with us & so on. It is not all gain commanding an expedition of this sort.*' In the event, there was a heart-stopping moment when two of the Sherpas were carried away by an incipient avalanche, but miraculously they were able to stop themselves. Outstanding rope work by Somervell completed the rescue, and all returned safely to Camp III, whence the entire expedition, exhausted, withdrew to Camp I.

THE SUMMIT ATTEMPTS

After a rest that left them revived, but by no means possessed of their full strength or health, the climbers gathered themselves on 29 May, ascension day, for a final attempt. A spell of better weather proved that the monsoon had not, as they feared, already arrived. The climbing strategy was reworked hastily, it was decided (or so they intended) to dispense entirely with the unsatisfactory oxygen, and two summit parties of two climbers each advanced up the mountain above the North Col to establish camps V and VI. The first of these two parties, Mallory and Geoffrey Bruce, established Camp V but were obliged to turn back at no very great altitude by their porters' sickness and uncharacteristic failure of morale in the face of the terrible wind. Bruce's heart was strained after this experience, and he was not fit for any further high-altitude work.

The second party consisted of Teddy and Howard Somervell. Teddy had convinced himself that only the highest possible camp siting would give a summit party a sporting chance. After his 1922 experience he believed that two camps above the North Col were essential, and that for the higher of them even 27,000 feet was too low. However it proved almost impossible to find at these altitudes a sufficiently level platform, even for a tiny two-man tent. Eventually the best they could do was to pitch camp at just under 27,000 feet. That done, they sent their small band of porters back down the mountain to Camp IV.

The two climbers spent the night of 3 June in Camp VI. Despite their weakness and the thinness of the atmosphere, they passed a good night. Later, in a letter to Younghusband, Teddy reported that '*I slept really well at 27,000 feet, and one will expect everyone to do so in future*'. The contrast with the physiologists' beliefs of only three years earlier is striking. His enjoyment of a good night's sleep was, however, marred on waking by the discovery that a thermos flask of hot tea, kept with him overnight in his sleeping bag, had lost its stopper and shed its contents – '*no longer warm*'. Precious time had to be wasted collecting more snow and reboiling a kettle.[3]

The weather on 4 June was excellent, with clear skies and an absence of the terrible wind that made high-altitude climbing on Everest such purgatory, though it was still bitterly cold. Their preferred route, traversing diagonally across the north face of the mountain below – but parallel to – the north-east ridge, would involve crossing the mighty snow-filled gully that plunges all the way down the face. This gully was called by the early expeditions the Great Couloir, though among some Everest climbers, including various Chinese expeditions, it has become

3 This episode might explain why seventy-seven years later, in 2001, when an Everest expedition rediscovered the site of the 1924 Camp VI, among the remains found there was a sock, which presumably had been discarded because it was soaked, with the nametape 'Norton' sewn into it.

known as the Norton Couloir. Once across the couloir, the climbers would be on the last leg, the final summit pyramid.

The rate of progress for climbers without oxygen at these extreme altitudes was agonisingly slow. From the start of the day, they were taking three to four complete respirations after every step, and before long this increased to ten. Even allowing for rapid panting, this was an exceedingly slow pace. They set themselves a target to advance twenty continuous steps without stopping, but never achieved more than thirteen before pausing to *'rest and pant elbow on bent knee.'* As Teddy later wrote, *'Somervell and I were only crawling.'* Nor did the calm weather save them from the effects of cold. The diary describes *'weather more or less windless but so cold that one shivered continually despite layers of windproof clothing, & when in sun.'*

The face on which they were climbing was formed of overlapping slabs of rock not unlike the overlapping tiles of a roof. Initially at a gentle gradient, which he described as giving *'excellent walking, hardly to be classed as climbing',* they eventually steepened and sloped outwards at a dangerous angle. There was no security whatever, and a slip would have been impossible to check. Teddy's many years of experience on the loose, steep shale surrounding the Chalet had been an ideal preparation for the top of Everest. Their progress was, however, further hampered by Somervell's severe high-altitude cough, and eventually he could go no further. He had to stop and sit down, and Teddy continued alone, towards the Great Couloir.

His own published account, in *The Fight for Everest 1924*, of this final solitary climb cannot be bettered:

> *'The going became a great deal worse; the slope was very steep below me, the foothold ledges narrowed to a few inches in width, and as I approached the shelter of the big couloir there*

was a lot of powdery snow that concealed the precarious footholds … I had twice to retrace my steps and follow a different band of strata; the couloir itself was filled with powdery snow into which I sank to the knee or even to the waist, and which was yet not of a consistency to support me in the event of a slip. Beyond the couloir the going got steadily worse; I found myself stepping from tile to tile, as it were, each tile sloping smoothly and steeply downwards; I began to feel that I was too much dependent on the mere friction of a boot nail on the slabs. It was not exactly difficult going, but it was a dangerous place for a single unroped climber, as one slip would have sent me in all probability to the bottom of the mountain. The strain of climbing so carefully was beginning to tell and I was getting exhausted. In addition my eye trouble was getting worse and was by now a severe handicap. I had perhaps 200 feet more of this nasty going to surmount before I emerged onto the north face of the final pyramid and, I believe, safety and an easy route to the summit. It was now 1 p.m., and a brief calculation showed that I had no chance of climbing the remaining 800 or 900 feet if I was to return in safety. At a point subsequently fixed by theodolite as 28,126 feet I turned back and retraced my steps to rejoin Somervell …

'*I feel that I ought to record the bitter feeling of disappointment which I should have experienced on having to acknowledge defeat with the summit so close; yet I cannot conscientiously say that I felt it much at the time. Twice now I have had thus to turn back on a favourable day when success had appeared possible, yet on neither occasion did I feel the sensations appropriate to the moment. This I think is a psychological*

*effect of great altitudes; the better qualities of ambition and
will to conquer seem dulled to nothing, and one turns
downhill with but little feelings other than relief that the
strain and effort of climbing are finished.'*

So ended his epic climb. Together the two climbers crept down the
mountain by the afternoon light and then in the gathering dusk, aiming
for Camp IV where a support party awaited them. To reach it took
them seven and a half hours in all. At the end, their approach to the
North Col was in complete darkness and by torchlight. A little higher
up, shortly after sunset, a final drama had taken place. Somervell's
cough and swollen larynx became so bad that he sat down, completely
unable to breathe and believing himself at the point of death, while
his companion, unaware of his predicament, hurried on down towards
the camp. Eventually Somervell was able to clear the obstruction in
his throat, coughing up a part of his throat lining together with the
obstruction, and they both reached the camp safely.

During the night, Teddy, who earlier in the day had removed his
snow goggles because he couldn't see his footing clearly, was struck
by painful snow blindness. He remained unable to see, and in acute
pain, for three days, at the end of which, though his sight was restored,
the expedition doctor told him that his heart was dilated – 'pretty rotten',
the diary comments.

It is worth pausing to reflect on his achievement. He had reached,
without using oxygen, an altitude, within 1,000 feet of the top of Everest,
that was not exceeded anywhere by any other oxygen-less climber for
fifty-four years, though in 1933 Wager, Wyn Harris and Smythe reached
approximately the same height. George Mallory and Sandy Irvine may
have – it is not certain – exceeded this altitude in 1924, but using oxygen.
Not until 1978 was his altitude record without oxygen exceeded, and

Everest climbed without oxygen to the summit, by Reinhold Messner and Peter Habeler. Summiting Everest without oxygen remains to this day an unusual accomplishment.

Specialists in high-altitude physiology have admired his achievement. The distinguished physiologist, and Himalayan climber, John West, in his book *High Life – a History of High-Altitude Physiology and Medicine*, cites Teddy's performance as outstanding within its time frame, and believes that survival at these altitudes without supplementary oxygen is clearly at the absolute limit of human capabilities. He discusses in his book whether top performers at high altitudes have unusual physical characteristics, but concludes 'that elite extreme-altitude climbers do not have readily identifiable physiological adaptations that can explain their unique performance. Exceptional motivation, and an incredible obsession to succeed, may be more important factors.'

Reflecting perhaps the same conclusion, Somervell, in a letter to Teddy's widow many years later, commented that:

> 'He was not the right physique for a long climb, being tall and spare – but he simply made himself do it with his strong and valiant mind, and got higher than anyone else though several including myself were of tougher build, and we all were failures by the side of Teddy who had more "guts" than any of us.'

Teddy himself believed that his only unusual physical characteristic was an abnormally slow pulse rate, and it is doubtful whether this was a significant advantage in a medical sense, though it is true that fit athletes in general have slow pulses.

He also believed from his own experience that, in good weather and with climbers in the peak of condition, there was no reason why Everest should not be climbed without resort to oxygen. This belief, and his actual performance, made its mark on later generations. Reinhold Messner, possibly the greatest climber of all, in his book *Everest – Expedition to the Ultimate* referred to Teddy as 'the Everest pioneer who has strongly influenced my thinking … It is true that E.F. Norton in his day believed that success without oxygen apparatus was possible, and had written that he could see no reason why a well-trained, fully-acclimatised man should not climb Everest without oxygen assistance … Whenever I find the time I reread Norton's account of his and Somervell's attempt in 1924.'

Stephen Venables, the first British climber to summit Everest without oxygen, in an epic climb in 1988, and a past president of the Alpine Club, wrote in a letter to my brother Bill,

'your father's amazingly bold attempt in 1924 was an important source of inspiration. We kept reminding ourselves that Norton had reached 28,000 feet in 1924, and insisted that with the right conditions it would have been possible to continue without oxygen … You probably know that in 1984 a small Australian team climbed the "North Face Direct" without oxygen. Their top camp was near the top of the Great Couloir. Nevertheless it took them a whole day to reach the summit from there. They found the exit out of the top right hand corner of the couloir [the point at which Teddy turned back] extremely precarious … Both we and the Australians found ourselves pushed right to the edge doing the climb without oxygen – not the sort of risks I'd like to take every day – and we were using vastly improved equipment and clothing. It made me appreciate the incredible courage of those pre-war attempts.'

When the Norton/Somervell duo returned exhausted to Camp IV, George Mallory, burning with ambition and deeply disappointed by the failure of his attempt with Bruce, had determined to have one more go at the summit, using oxygen (notwithstanding the earlier decision). He had chosen as his climbing companion the relatively inexperienced climber, but excellent oxygen practitioner, Sandy Irvine. Teddy, suffering acutely from snow blindness, felt in no position to debate Mallory's change of plan, and in any case he had agreed to defer to Mallory as the expedition's climbing leader.

The story of Mallory and Irvine's attempt, and how it ended in their tragic disappearance, has been told far too many times for me to repeat it in any detail. Mallory planned to take his favoured route, the northeast ridge, above and parallel to the Norton/Somervell route. This would involve confronting and overcoming the Second Step, a hazard that some of the expedition members doubted it was feasible to climb.

They set out from the highest camp on the morning of 8 June, in weather inferior to that on 4 June, in that cloud came and went across the face of the mountain, accompanied by snow flurries. After that, almost nothing is known of their progress for sure. Odell, following behind them in support lower down the mountain, had a brief glimpse of them in a break in the cloud, apparently climbing the Second Step successfully. But even that is inconclusive evidence, since he could not be certain that the location of the sighting was in fact the Second Step. Certainly the time of his sighting, 12.50 p.m., was a long way too late for them to be at that point in their ascent, unless there had been some serious delay in their progress lower down. Whatever the explanation of that, they were never seen again. Odell made a second visit to their high camp on the following day in case there was any trace of them. From Camp III, with the onset of the monsoon threatening ominously, Teddy sent on the 9 June an instruction to Odell and Hazard at Camp

IV that only a limited further search should be attempted, and (from the diary) *'Principle to risk no more lives in trying to retrieve the inevitable'.* By the time 10 June arrived, there was no alternative for the expedition and its leader but to conclude that Mallory and Irvine had been lost for good.

The dramatic and sobering discovery of Mallory's body – lying low on the slopes of the north face – by the expedition led by Eric Simonson in 1999, caused a painstaking re-examination of the evidence for and against the hypothesis that he and Irvine had reached the summit in 1924. It was clear, for instance, that they had died as the result of a climbing accident rather than from exposure and hypothermia, since the rope tied round Mallory's waist was broken and frayed a short distance from his body.

The results of this debate, which are thus far still inconclusive, are admirably summarised in Jochen Hemmleb and Eric Simonson's 2002 book *Detectives on Everest*. Their account sums up the evidence thus,

> 'they could have reached the top – which is still a far cry from saying that they did … No matter how inconceivable one thinks it might be, the incomplete and conflicting evidence has to allow for the chance that they made it … Perhaps one day the mountain will reveal additional pieces of the puzzles to complete the picture of Mallory and Irvine's final day. Until then, nobody will know for certain what happened on June 8, 1924.'

Teddy's own view, that their deaths were almost certainly the result of a climbing accident rather than death from exposure after being benighted, was entirely vindicated by the 1999 discovery. He was equally convinced that Mallory would never have taken a 'death or glory' attitude to conquering Everest at all costs (or risks). In an address to the RGS and Alpine Club after the expedition, he said, *'At the same time those who suggest that he may have taken chances to achieve success in his last climb* misrepresent him. *For equally strong as his will to conquer was his sense of responsibility as leader of a party, and I know that he was prepared – nay, determined – to turn back, however near the summit, if it could not be reached in time to return in safety.'* To Mallory's widow, he wrote in similar vein, *'He and I saw eye-to-eye over the question of the absolute necessity of avoiding a single casualty even to conquer the mountain – and he has often told me his views as to the point at which the leader of a party must turn back for safety's sake however near the goal.'*

The long wait for confirmation of Mallory and Irvine's fate, the eventual conclusion that they had died, and the subsequent digesting of the expedition's failure and loss of life, he found very dispiriting. Of his moment of realisation, while waiting at Camp III, that they must have met their deaths, he wrote in his diary, *'Of all the truly miserable days I have spent at III this by far the worst – by now it appears almost inevitable that disaster has overtaken poor gallant Mallory and Irvine – 10 to 1 they have 'fallen off' high up.'* A week later, he wrote in low spirits to Younghusband, *'Now that we have done with the mountain, in spite of your confidence in me I have nothing to report but failure and disaster. I can assure you that none of you* [the committee] *can be more disappointed than I am.'* Writing to Irvine's parents, he says, *'To me the whole thing is very bitter, my fixed determination was to bring off success if possible, but, success or failure, above all things to avoid casualties – and I thought it could be done. I was determined that such splendid lives as those we have lost were infinitely too high a price to pay for success.'*

So ended the 1924 expedition. Writing many years later for the *Geographical Journal*, Eric Shipton, himself a distinguished Everest climber in the ensuing decade, summed it up in a single sentence. 'The story of that expedition is one of extraordinary perseverance in the face of crushing misfortune, of outstanding achievement against heavy odds, of success so nearly grasped and, finally, of tragedy.' In 1953, during his return from the expedition that successfully reached the summit of Everest, Sir John Hunt wrote, in a letter to Teddy:

'I would also like you to know how very much you and the 1924 expedition have been in our minds during recent months. We have always regarded your team as a model which we should emulate; as you know, we have throughout been very conscious of the huge debt which we owed to you and to others who have gone before us. To you goes a big share in the glory.'

As for Teddy himself, he emerged from it with distinction in two senses. His record achievement as a high-altitude climber has already been described. But hardly less notable was the quality of his leadership. Pitched into the role unexpectedly by the accident of General Bruce's illness, he conducted it in a way that aroused admiration at the time. The account of the expedition speaks for itself, and I have quoted in a previous chapter Howard Somervell's views, and Michael Ward's – 'probably the best of all Everest leaders'. Occasionally entries in his diary let slip the pressures he felt, and the internal agonising that a conscientious leader must experience. '*Indifferent night – head too full of the very apparent difficulties and dangers of the whole business. I slept little thinking of most unpleasant job ahead of us … It is not all gain commanding an expedition of this sort.*'

A feature of his leadership, one often overlooked, was the trouble he took to get to know as many as possible of the porters, by name, character and background. The personal interest he took in them and their welfare becomes clear from a careful reading of the chapters written by him in the two published accounts of these early expeditions, *The Assault on Everest 1922* and *The Fight for Everest 1924*. It undoubtedly

helped him (together with his language skills) to influence the performance of the 'Tigers', the leading Sherpas who carried loads to the highest
altitudes, at one or two critical moments as events unfolded.

Writing to him towards the end of the expedition, Arthur Hinks says
in his letter of 26 June:

> 'What strikes us all in contrast to the events of 1922 is the
> magnificent leadership and organisation of the whole thing,
> by which everyone supported everyone else … Whatever
> Hingston proved to you scientifically about deterioration of
> the brain at high altitudes, you have routed him triumphantly
> by showing a fine grip of circumstances as any man could have
> shown. Let me congratulate you especially upon your dispatch
> of June 8 from Camp III – dictated when you were snow
> blinded to a secretary [Geoff Bruce] with a strained heart.
> It was a superb performance.'

And again on 2 July,

> 'I would like to emphasise the universally expressed
> admiration for your leadership in those thrilling ten days.'

Teddy replied to this in his letter of 19 July, with typical modesty.

> *'I think you give me too much credit for the organisation we
> have been able to put into the business this year – for you must
> not forget that two years ago, we were all groping with but
> little knowledge of where we were going next, while this year
> we stood on the shoulders of the 1922 expedition so to speak.
> Further, I got the most magnificent backing from Mallory,*

Geoff Bruce and Somervell. The first the most indefatigable worker with an astonishing power of application to detail, the second absolute king of the native personnel (I don't know how a future expedition could ever dispense with him), the third possessed of about the quickest and clearest brain I know. So think of the 1924 expedition in future as a combination of the above most efficient elements – emphatically not a one man show.'

THE AFTERMATH

Various things flowed from the Everest expeditions in his later life. In the winter of 1923–1924, the International Olympic Committee had awarded the 1922 expedition members Olympic gold medals, and at the insistence of the climbers these were extended also to a number of the Tigers. Teddy was awarded the RGS's gold Founder's Medal in 1926, and elected to its council, of which he remained a member until his departure for India at the end of the decade. In addition, having been elected to the Alpine Club while a member of the 1922 expedition, he was twice in later years approached by the committee of the club to accept high office. In 1943 he was offered the vice presidency, but declined it from modesty about his climbing accomplishments. In 1946 he was again approached, this time to accept the presidency. His letter of reply protests his inadequacy for the honour, and presses the committee to find someone better qualified. *'My decision therefore is to place myself in your hands and those of the committee. I feel it would be ungracious to do otherwise, but I do hope that you will believe that I am not actuated by an access of false modesty or anything of that sort, and will weigh what I have written very seriously against the qualifications of other possible starters.'* In the end, and with considerable reluctance, the committee deferred to his unwillingness and offered the post to Tom Longstaff, a decision that must have given him great pleasure.

He was also considered as a serious candidate for leadership of two of the later Everest expeditions, in 1933 and 1935, but the demands of his military career took precedence. He was however regularly consulted for his advice and experience as the later Everest expeditions were mounted, by Hugh Ruttledge in 1933 and 1936, by Eric Shipton in 1952, and by Sir John Hunt before the first successful ascent of Everest in 1953. Hunt, in his published account *The Ascent of Everest*, pays tribute to the importance of Teddy's advice that the final assault camp should be sited as high as possible on the mountain. As late as 1950, twenty-six years after his high climb, he wrote for the *Alpine Journal* a lengthy appraisal of the prospects for surmounting the 'last thousand feet' via his route across the north face and the Great Couloir. The article contains detailed insights into the terrain he had crossed after leaving Somervell, and underlines the acute difficulties posed by the couloir and the slopes beyond it. Even at that date, it was still assumed that the mountain would be climbed from the north, though in the event the first ascent, only three years later, and many ensuing expeditions used the entirely different southern approach through Nepal.

One curious outcome of his temporary celebrity from the 1924 expedition was the naming of a mountain in the Canadian Rockies after him, in 1927. The American climber Alfred Ostheimer, who was making a series of first ascents in a previously unclimbed range, called two of his peaks Mount Norton (with a height of 10,200 feet) and Mount Somervell. Both names were accepted by mapmakers, and are still used.

In spite of his notable Himalayan achievements in the 1920s, he did not go on to attempt a string of other great Himalayan or Alpine climbs. He was always first and foremost a soldier, and mountaineering was not for him an end in itself, but a highly enjoyable pastime, to be savoured whenever possible in his leisure time. He continued with a few classic Alpine routes in the late 1920s, and in the 1930s climbed mountains in

Scotland or in north-west India whenever he got the chance. He jealously nurtured his fitness on these excursions, and would record his times for altitude gain in his sporting diaries. '*21.2.30, on my 46th birthday, and after not being on a hill for 4 months, climbed 2500 ft on Murdar* [near Quetta, in what is now Pakistan] *in an hour going quite easily. Cf. 24.3.27*'. This last refers back to his diary entry of that date while in Scotland, '*Went up Ben Lawers. 3500 feet in 1 hr 28 mins.*' This, he used to say, was his fastest-ever uphill speed on any mountain. It is roughly ten times faster than he achieved on the day of his high climb in 1924.

He continued climbing or hillwalking until well into his sixties, latterly in Scotland for the most part, where, on at least one occasion, his adult and teenage sons could barely match his pace uphill. In 1949, aged sixty-five, while visiting the Norton estancia in Argentina, he walked up a local peak called Curumalan Grande, and his wife took a charming photograph of him resting on the summit, binoculars in hand, gazing at the distant view. This was to be his last mountain. On his return from Argentina, the onset of poor health put a final stop to his mountaineering.

Four Norton brothers at the Chalet around 1910; from left, Teddy, Gen, Jack and Dick.

Joyce, a studio portrait, 1941.

5

THE MIDDLE YEARS

MARRIAGE AND FAMILY LIFE

The four-year period between December 1921, when Teddy left staff college, and January 1926, when he began a two-year assignment at the War Office in London, was interrupted by the two Everest expeditions. Each took up six to seven months, and as a result he had no lengthy appointments in this period. Six weeks at the start of 1922 were spent on a gunnery course at Larkhill. The months from October 1922 to August 1923 he spent at Chanak. From September 1923 to February 1924 he had a temporary appointment at the War Office. On return from the 1924 Everest expedition, he took up in September 1924, with the rank of lieutenant colonel, command of a pack battery (21st Light Battery RA) at Norwich, but this too lasted only until December 1925, after which his two-year tour at the War Office began.

In spite of this, his career progression from 1926 until the late 1930s shows that his prospects had certainly not been damaged by the series of short-term postings. More important, however, in every way than these soldiering episodes was the turning point of 1925, the year in which he became engaged, and then married, to Joyce Pasteur, and entered into the role of a family man. This would bring a totally new dimension to his life.

Isabel Joyce Pasteur came from a family which, on her father's side, was closely linked to the Wills family (see family tree in appendices) and the tradition of early alpine climbing. Her grandfather, Henri Pasteur, a Genevese (and therefore French-speaking) Swiss, was a contemporary and friend of Alfred Wills, and a fellow member of the pioneering generation of alpine mountaineers. He and his Genevese wife Caroline were among the circle of friends that Wills liked to surround himself with at the summer gatherings at the Chalet, and this tradition passed down to the succeeding generations. Henri and Caroline were Anglophiles, and in midlife they left their native Geneva and relocated themselves to England, later taking British nationality.

Their son William, Joyce's father, inherited the climbing bug from his father, and became in due course an experienced alpine climber, and an Alpine Club member who on his death merited a substantial obituary in the *Alpine Journal*, written by Teddy. He also became a successful and distinguished doctor, specialising in paediatrics and in particular respiratory illnesses, and consulting at some of the major London hospitals from his home in Chandos Street. His distinction in the medical world was reflected in his election to the presidency of the Medical Society of London in 1915. He had great personal charm. In his leisure hours he was a keen gardener and a skilled carpenter. In his retirement he created jigsaw puzzles, which were beautifully crafted and are works of art in their own right. Joyce liked to refer to herself, with some pride, as a doctor's daughter, and had a warm affection for her father.

William married Violet Sellon, described by Joyce as a great beauty in her youth, a gentle and artistic soul whom I remember in her old age as an archetypal 'sweet old lady'. She was a direct descendant of a minor hero of the First Afghan War, Lieutenant Thomas Souter, who in 1842 led the last surviving remnants of the 44th Regiment of Foot in the final moments of their disastrous slaughter at Gandamak, from which he was hustled away wounded, and for some months kept a prisoner by the Afghans in hopes of a ransom – which was not paid. William and Violet had three children, a son and two daughters, of whom Joyce was the youngest, born in 1900, and thus sixteen years younger than Teddy. Her brother Raymond became, like Teddy's brother Dick, a casualty of the First World War, killed in action in Flanders in 1917. She herself spent time during the war, as a teenager, nursing the war wounded in London hospitals.

The Pasteurs and their daughters, in particular Joyce, were frequent guests at the Chalet parties, which Joyce began to attend from the age of eleven upwards. She would have got to know Teddy there, as an older man whom she may at first have regarded with a degree of awe. She had a good aptitude as a climber, and later joined some of Geoffrey Winthrop Young's celebrated climbing parties in Snowdonia. Teddy visited the Chalet briefly on his return from Everest in September 1924, but was quickly summoned back to duty in Norwich. So in the summer of 1925 he returned to the Chalet intending a longer stay there, together with his mother and brothers. Joyce Pasteur was also included in the party.

Aged twenty-five, she was a well-built young woman, tall for her generation – a fraction short of five-foot-nine – and perhaps better described as handsome rather than pretty. She was quick-witted and intelligent and had a lively personality, but also a streak of pragmatism that stood her in good stead in a life of varied experiences, and she shared many of Teddy's enthusiasms. He must have seen her, over the years, maturing gradually to become a fully grown young lady. He may have been suddenly smitten by a *coup de foudre*, or he may have nursed a fancy for her for a while, but in any event on 18 August he chose a romantic locale, by a favourite mountain lake above the Chalet, to propose to her. She accepted him then and there. Indeed, her own version of the event was that he led her uphill to the chosen spot at such a cracking pace, and then proposed to her so quickly after she had sat down, that she was too out of breath even to say no. After a short engagement, they were married on 18 December of the same year at St George's Hanover Square in London, and the new era of married life began for Teddy.[1]

At the time of their marriage he was forty-one and she was twenty-five, but the difference in age, perhaps less uncommon at that time than it would be now, was never an obstacle or an issue between them. He wrote to her during their engagement, with his usual wry humour, that his elder brother Jack and his wife Madge, themselves already married for sixteen years, *'won't hear of it that it's a shame for a girl like you to marry a man so old as I am – on the contrary, they seem to have some doubts as to whether I am sufficiently grown up to marry.'* Other letters written to his fiancée at this time convey his huge delight and surprise at the new experience of being in love. *'I do believe I'm in for such happiness as I've never known before, though I've always regarded myself as the happiest man I ever knew … I was beginning to realise what a miserable prospect was ahead of me – out of tune with post war mess life – hating above all things club life … To think that I should write such letters – pages and pages without anything about my battery or my sport or any of the things I used to write about.'* And three weeks later, *'you've made me suddenly begin to wonder whether my next 40 years (for I shall certainly live to 80) isn't going to be far better than the last 40 – and they were magnificent – instead of being a miserable existence as a "professional uncle".'*

---

1 To celebrate his marriage, Teddy commissioned the building of a mountain hut in the Vallée des Fonds, on a much higher vantage point that overlooked the Chalet. Known as the Collet Chalet, this rapidly became a great favourite with the Nortons for their excursions into the higher regions.

He did not, alas, live to eighty, and Joyce was only fifty-four when he died. Herself eventually dying at ninety-two, she outlived him by thirty-eight years – for twenty-nine years a wife, for thirty-eight a widow. She, like her mother-in-law, was gradually transformed into a true matriarch, remembered with great affection by a wide spread of cousins, nephews and nieces as well as her children, grandchildren and great-grandchildren.

But that was all in the future, and we should return to 1925. As is the case with good marriages, Joyce brought to her union with Teddy not only shared enthusiasms, but also some new and complementary skills and interests. Like him, she was or at least became a capable horsewoman, had a passion for fishing and for mountains and mountain surroundings, and, although born and brought up in central London, took readily to life in the countryside. It was no accident that they chose for their honeymoon the mountainous island of Corsica, and their marriage drew a letter of approval from Winthrop Young, 'because it unites two of the great aristocracies of mountaineering'.

On the other hand, unlike her husband who was tone deaf, she had a fine musical ear, coming from the musically talented Pasteur clan, with a number of professional musicians among her cousins. She played the piano well, having studied it at the Royal College of Music, and had a strong, clear contralto voice. She became responsible for the musical element in their children's upbringing. She was also a good gardener with a wide knowledge of cultivated plants, which Teddy deferred to, his own botanical expertise being strictly in the sphere of wild flowers, shrubs and trees. She had her own range of literary and theatrical tastes. And, unlike the Norton family, close-knit at the nuclear level but having only sporadic contact with their cousins and the extended family, she belonged to a broad, strong network of cousins who exhibited the Swiss tradition of clannishness. My brothers and I were, in consequence, brought up in frequent contact with numerous first, second and occasionally third cousins on the Pasteur side of the family.

The marriage produced three sons, though they both hoped for at least one daughter. Dick was born in 1926, Bill in 1933 and Hugh, the author of this book, in 1936. That they all had one-syllable everyday names was no accident. Teddy joked that he didn't want to waste his breath every time he had to yell for them. He made the transition from confirmed bachelor to proud father and family man quickly and easily. He devoted more time than many fathers to teaching his sons his enthusiasm for the sports, skills, interests and pastimes that had meant so much to him. Other than shooting game, he succeeded in passing on virtually all his tastes and likings to one or more of his sons, so that, for instance, Dick became an accomplished horseman, and Bill a skilled watercolourist and keen ornithologist. I shall write more about this in a later chapter.

SOLDIERING IN ENGLAND

So began the second and, at a personal level, very different half of Teddy's life. And at the same time as he embarked on the married state, he also resumed a steady progression through the stages of his career as a peacetime soldier, building on his wartime experiences and the succession of short-term appointments around the time of the Everest expeditions. This phase began in January 1926, directly after the wedding, with a full-length staff appointment, all of four years since his graduation from staff college. His posting as a general staff officer grade II (GSO II) – usually a major's appointment but occasionally filled by a brevet lieutenant-colonel – in the Military Operations Directorate of the War Office in London was something of a pat on the back. Military Operations was generally regarded as an elite directorate in the War Office. Its responsibilities – mainly the strategic direction of land-based operations worldwide – were discharged by several branches, each responsible for a specific region. Teddy was assigned to the branch dealing with the Far East including, intriguingly in the light of his later experiences, Hong Kong.

In those days, and indeed until well after The Second World War, the War Office, overseeing the army, was one of three departments of government each concerned with a single armed service, and each one having a secretary of state with a seat in cabinet, the others being the Admiralty and the Air Ministry. Not until 1964 were the three separate departments fully amalgamated into a single Ministry of Defence. Staff officers in the War Office, even at a quite junior level, could expect to broaden their experience by contributing to national policy formulation and high-level committee work, which involved civil servants and even occasionally ministers. Many found the change from straightforward soldiering unwelcome, including Teddy, but experience of working in a government department is more or less essential for those destined for the higher rungs of the career ladder. In spite of the considerable workload, Teddy managed to get away for the best part of a day per week, on average, to hunt with the Pytchley Hunt, making up for time out of the office by working late in the evenings.

The appointment lasted exactly two years, and the newlyweds found themselves accommodation at Catherine Street in Buckingham Gate. On 19 November 1926, their first son Dick, baptised Richard Pasteur, was born at a nursing home in Welbeck Street, and a month later they engaged a young live-in nanny called Ruth Vockins. This arrangement succeeded well enough for 'Nannie', as she was called by all the family, to remain a fixed part of the household for twenty-eight years. She accompanied them to all the places where the family later moved in pursuit of Teddy's career, shuttling back and forth between England and Quetta, Ziarat, Ootacamund and Bangalore in India, and Cape Town in South Africa.

His next appointment after the War Office, starting in January 1928, was as a student at the Imperial Defence College. This was a recently created establishment for the education of more senior officers from all three services and their counterparts in Commonwealth armed forces, together with a few civil servants and diplomats, in defence studies of a broad strategic nature. The college opened its gates to students for the first time in 1927, so Teddy was a member of only the second intake. Minutes of the chiefs of staff sub-committee of the Committee of Imperial Defence show that the concept was, at the outset, both experimental and ambitious. The students were taken through 'studies of hypothetical war' and 'studies of the general principles of defence and organisation for war'. A report to the sub-committee from Admiral Richmond, the first commandant of the college, described how 'an attempt had been made to produce a paper expressing in broad outline the governing principles for imperial defence. No satisfactory paper however has been produced, and the problem will be studied again.'

The 'schemes and appreciations' undertaken in the early courses included principles of war, principles of imperial defence, and higher direction of war. They also included the British Empire and Japan – Teddy's future was again casting a long shadow. The emphasis on the Commonwealth as the focus of war studies gradually faded from prominence over the years, and attendance by officers from Commonwealth armed forces seems to have been lower than expected even from the beginning. Eventually, in 1970, the college was renamed the Royal College of Defence Studies, and opened its doors to students from a much wider range of countries, including China, Russia, Pakistan and Zimbabwe over the ensuing years.

The total number of students at the first year's course was twenty-five, and as late as 1938 had only risen to thirty-six. Even after the widening of the remit by the Royal College of Defence Studies, student numbers were typically less than 100. The fact is that the students were hand-picked high-flyers, selected on the strength of their potential to advance to the highest positions in their various organisations, and invited to acquire a broad knowledge of defence and international security, and an understanding of strategic vision at the highest level. Teddy, who fitted this specification, was aged forty-three when he joined the college, at or a little below the median age of the students. Without doubt it was a feather in his cap to be chosen for the second course run by the fledgling college.

BACK TO NORTHERN INDIA

Although the college was located in Belgravia in central London, he and his family moved for the year 1928, for reasons that are obscure, from London to Camberley. It was from there that they left, in January 1929, to embark on the troopship *Nevasa* bound for Karachi. From Karachi they went upcountry to Quetta in Baluchistan, not far from the Afghan border, where Teddy had been appointed as a senior instructor at the Quetta staff college. This was the counterpart in India of the college at Camberley, at which students coming from both the Indian Army and the British Army in India were taught. Promotion to full colonel coincided with the appointment. For the most part, his duties involved the management of the directing staff who taught the senior division of students. He evidently took the rapid progression from student to senior instructor in his stride, to judge from his confidential reports at the time – 'not only is his military knowledge above the average but he has the knack to impart it'. He was, however, not immune from carelessness. One minor mishap occurred when he lost his list of the students in a new intake, which he had annotated, as an aide-memoire to identification, with brief notes describing their most unflattering facial features. It never turned up. He had committed a similar faux pas when at the War Office, leaving a highly confidential document in a taxi. Luckily that too disappeared without trace, and without repercussions for him.

By now his career was becoming increasingly focused on India, indeed he was already something of an India specialist. This focus would continue with further and later postings. Quetta however, and the North-West Frontier in which it lay, was unfamiliar to him. It sits in relatively arid terrain in the foothills of the ranges that mark the border with Afghanistan. It is surrounded by hills, and a number of higher mountains that punctuate the skyline. And lying close to a tectonic plate boundary, it is earthquake-prone. Between his first and second postings to Quetta, the town suffered a devastating earthquake in 1935, which destroyed the town centre almost entirely, and killed an estimated 50,000 people. It was a largely reconstructed place, with a very different appearance, on his return there in 1940.

He soon developed a liking for the local people of the area, with their forthright Muslim character, which he found more to his taste than the Hindu southerners of Madras District that he was to meet a few years later. (His initial acquaintance with his house servants in Bangalore in 1938 provoked the comment, in a letter to Joyce, that they 'simply won't do after the nice up country mahomedans' – though later he warmed to the southerners, and made some loyal friends among them.) While in Quetta he found scope for his sporting pursuits. He made a beeline for the mountains, climbing Takatu and Murdar, the two pre-eminent peaks visible from Quetta, within a few months of his arrival. And he hunted with hounds – the British had brought this sport with them, though the quarry was normally jackals not foxes – and occasionally indulged his love of pig-sticking. A curious episode linked hunting with earthquakes. He was following the hunt one day and came to a nullah (a small, steep-sided ravine) crossing his path.

Horse and rider took off to jump across the nullah, and as they were in mid-air, an earthquake struck, so that when they hit the ground on the far side, the earth was shaking violently. Whatever the horse thought of this, it certainly made an impact on Teddy.

In Baluchistan the Norton family led a fairly calm and uneventful life, having friends and family to stay, exploring Kashmir on their holidays, and entirely escaping the gloom of the Great Depression in Britain, which more or less coincided with their three years in Quetta. For relief from the heat of the summer, they could resort for short periods to the village of Ziarat in the forested higher regions, where the British Raj had built one of its characteristic hill stations for rest and relaxation.

THE ALDERSHOT YEARS

Returning to England with the family in the spring of 1932, at the end of the three-year posting, he was delighted to get back once more to a command appointment, after a six-year spell on the staff and at staff colleges. He was promoted brigadier and took up the post of commander royal artillery (CRA) of the 1st Division at Aldershot. Thus, leaving aside his intervening staff and training appointments, he had leapfrogged from command of a battery – the 21st Light Battery at Norwich – to the command of several gunner regiments, omitting the key stage of commanding a single regiment as a lieutenant colonel. This was a very unusual career jump, bearing witness to his high-flyer status and the high regard in which he was held. It was an important period professionally, coinciding with the artillery's transition from horse-drawn to mechanised status.

The family lived in an army quarter near Farnham for the duration of the appointment, which lasted a little over two years. In his confidential report in 1933, his immediate superior wrote,

'a very outstanding officer in every respect with all the
attributes of a great commander … Considerably above
the average of his rank',

and the comment from a more senior level came from none other than
General Harrington, who was mentioned earlier as the commanding
general in the Chanak affair:

'I agree. Undoubtedly one of the best officers in the army.
I knew him in the war in the Canadian Corps, he served under
me in Turkey and I knew him as an instructor in the QSC and
I know his work here. He has a most charming personality.
He is always one to help others and is liked by all.'

In the middle of this period, he had to bear for the third time the death
of a brother younger than himself. Gen, the youngest of the three close-
knit Norton brothers, had married much earlier than Teddy, and already
had three young children. He had opted for a career in the Royal Navy,
which had taken him to assignments in South Africa (his wife was
South African), but had been invalided out of the navy, having suffered
damage to his eardrums from naval gunfire. Later he took up farming in
Rhodesia. He did not stay there for long, but returned to England, and
then went to live in Switzerland.

Lively and adventurous by nature, he earned a reputation for impet-
uosity, both in his business dealings and in his sporting activities. For a
long time he had been a keen skier as well as mountaineer, preferring
the cross-country version of the sport to downhill. In March 1933, while
skiing on a mountainside above Sixt and near to the Chalet, and perhaps
taking unwise risks in tricky snow conditions, he was avalanched and
swept to his death. As well as suffering this close family bereavement,

Teddy was also deprived of the chance to learn skiing, as he had planned to do at the age of forty-nine. As he wrote later to his son Bill, '*My brother Gen always reckoned that this* [long trips off-piste] *was the real joy of skiing and not the technical proficiency needed for competitions and fancy work nearer your base. I had just invested in a pair of skiing boots and was going to join him and learn his game when he was killed. So I never went, and have never put on skis.*'

The Lord taketh away, and the Lord giveth. In September of the same year, Teddy's second son Bill was born, also at the nursing home in Welbeck Street, as Dick had been. The baby was baptised William John Eric, the last name in memory of Gen. The year before, 1932, had seen another and very different addition to the household. Teddy had assigned to him a soldier servant (batman), a gunner from Hertfordshire named Charlie Hancock, who stayed with him till 1938. Later, after the end of the Second World War, having been invalided out of the army on a disability pension, he offered his services to Teddy, also in retirement, and was taken on as a gardener and general factotum to the family in their new home near Winchester. Down-to-earth, hard working, talkative, and with a streak of sentimentality, he was a popular addition to the household. He remained intensely loyal to 'the general' up to his death, and indeed stayed with the Norton household for many years after.

In June 1934, Teddy reverted to another staff appointment, as brigadier general staff (BGS) to the Aldershot Command. Aldershot Command, despite being in essence a static sub-division of the home army alongside other commands, prided itself on being the senior command, containing the lion's share of the operational and functional units, and on having its headquarters in 'the home of the British Army', as Aldershot's town sign proclaimed. With unwelcome developments already stirring in Germany, coupled with the accelerating pace of army mechanisation, there was a distinct buzz about serving in the command headquarters. Teddy's job was in effect the principal staff officer to the general officer commanding-in-chief (C-in-C). He was quartered in the official residence that went with the job, Blandford House in Farnborough, whose grounds abutted on to those of Government House, the C-in-C's residence. So the family had to make the short move from Farnham to Farnborough.

Blandford House was an agreeable and comfortable family home with a fair-sized garden. At the end of the working day, in summer at least, Teddy enjoyed coaching Dick, by then rising eight, at cricket on the lawn until, with a resigned sigh, he would bowl the last ball and then head off to his study, or to a deckchair if the weather was fine, to catch up on office paperwork before changing for dinner.

This posting lasted nearly four years, until March 1938 – unusually long in comparison with most army postings, and a contrast with his earlier military career, in which he had scarcely exceeded two years in any one post since his very early days at Meerut. There is reason to believe that it marked the turning point at which his previously meteoric career began to plateau. He himself felt that this was the case, not least in the light of his two succeeding appointments to command two of the Indian districts, which, although they involved further promotion, left him deeply frustrated at being removed from the European theatre of action to what he perceived as a career backwater. From 1939 on, he particularly regretted never having the chance of operational command in a theatre of war.

One possible factor in this turn of fortune may have been his crossing swords with the C-in-C at Aldershot, General Sir Francis Gathorne-Hardy, for whose judgement in military matters he seems, on one occasion at least, to have had little respect. The story goes that he took issue publicly with the C-in-C over the latter's plans for, and conduct of, a high-level military exercise. He was overruled, but the upshot of the exercise proved that the C-in-C was in the wrong, and Gathorne-Hardy took umbrage at being shown up by a subordinate. Whether or not this contributed to the direction his career took cannot of course be proved one way or the other, and Gathorne-Hardy certainly wrote at least one very complimentary confidential report on him. But Teddy was not alone in regretting his next assignments in India. Jock Wedderburn-Maxwell, a gunner officer who had served under him and whose views have been quoted earlier, wrote of the tragedy of someone with his 'all-round brilliance and robust personality' being 'buried' in an Indian district at the start of the Second World War. His brother-in-law Wardrop also believed that he would have been destined for higher things, but for the accident of being in the wrong place at the wrong time.

The year 1936, like 1933, brought both loss and gain. The death of his mother Edith in August at the Chalet, at the age of eighty-one, has been described before. She remained up to the end in the place that she loved best of anywhere, and was buried in the churchyard at Sixt. Less than two months earlier, Joyce had given birth to their third son Hugh at the London Clinic in Harley Street. He was baptised Hugh Edward, thus carrying the Christian name of his father, grandfather and great-grandfather, a name which has been perpetuated in two subsequent generations of the family.

In 1937, Teddy was appointed aide-de-camp to King George VI, who had recently assumed the throne in succession to his brother. A small number of ADCs to the monarch from each of the services were appointed for a period of a year or more. The appointment was honorary, and was additional to, not in lieu of, his current job at Aldershot Command. The duties were mainly ceremonial, and the significance lay in the fact that it was considered an honour and accolade to be so appointed, rather than in any particular activity or service involved. The appointment lapsed on his transfer to his next assignment.

SOUTHERN INDIA – BANGALORE

In March 1938 his period as BGS Aldershot Command came to an end, and he was promoted to major general and dispatched to take command of Madras District, in southern India. This involved assuming authority over all the units in this district not only of the British Army in India and the Indian Army itself, which was, in the upper reaches, largely officered by British expatriates at this time, but also of the Auxiliary Force of India (AFI), a sort of Territorial Army of volunteers that could be mobilised in the event of an attack on the country. At this juncture, it was decided that Joyce and the children would remain behind in England for a few months, and that Teddy would proceed to India unaccompanied. The reason centred, for the most part, on Dick's education. He was at a critical time in his schooling at West Downs, a boarding prep-school in Winchester that was in part an incubator for Winchester College, to which the Norton parents aspired to send their children. The decision also gave Joyce the chance to be closer to, and see more of, her parents, who were becoming elderly and frail.

So Teddy sailed on his own to Bombay and landed there in April 1938. *'Bombay is rather more revolting than usual'* he wrote to Joyce about his arrival. From Bombay he proceeded to Bangalore, the location of his headquarters and residence, positioned centrally to his area of responsibility, but at some distance from Madras, the centre of civil government of the district. He was again unfamiliar with this part of India, and wasted no time in travelling around and getting to know the region. Madras District combined a variety of quite different landscape types, from lush coastal forest through dry inland jungles, arid desert terrain, and on to cool upland plateaus.

His activities as commander Madras District were a non-stop combination of ceremonial and social duties, a great deal of inspecting of military units and depots, administrative and managerial tasks, and a limited amount of training and military strategic planning, both of which he enjoyed. His duties involved, among other things, an invitation to visit the Nandidroog gold mine at Kolar to the east of Bangalore, then reputed to be the deepest mine in the world. During this inspection he descended to the bottom of the mine, carried for the last 2,000 feet of the descent in a sort of open bucket. Thus he gained the distinction of having stood at two points on earth separated by a greater vertical difference in altitude than any other human being until that time, and possibly since. This allowed him to quip, in a speech made at a boys' school the same year, that, while the mine had a lift to take him to the depths, unfortunately Mount Everest 'did not have that amenity'.

But most of these activities were not at all to his taste, as he made clear in some of his numerous letters to Joyce. Only a month after his arrival, he was writing, '*Time passes with leaden feet and so far I haven't had one spark of enjoyment out of life since we parted.*' After two months, '*You can imagine how I hate it all* ... [The constant social round] *makes me feel that about a year of this job after you get here will be enough for me. The soldiering is simply futile and wants at most a brigadier ... From day's end to day's end I never see a single face I want to see again ... Now that I've done with the initial interest of new country and new places there simply isn't a single thing to look forward to this side of October. Time seems to be literally standing still.*' And a week later: '*an endless series of social functions ... You can guess how I detest all this, but I simply accept it as part of my duty here, and unavoidable in a way that did not apply quite so strongly in Aldershot.*' His observation that the soldiering was unworthy of his rank was echoed by his superior General Brind, in his 1939 confidential report:

> 'An exceptionally able and versatile commander ... the number of regular troops that he has to train are insufficient to give full

scope to his ability and capacity. I recommend that he be considered for transfer to a first-class district.'

His unease was increased when he discovered very early signs that his eyesight was deteriorating. He first detected this on the tennis court. Perhaps for one aged fifty-four this should not have been such a surprise, but it troubled him considerably, and was a foretaste of the more serious eye trouble that would afflict him a decade or so later. '*It is a shock to find that my distant, or anyway middle-distant sight is going,*' he wrote, '*and I really don't know what to be at.*'

In spite of these bouts of low morale, he was active in the sporting sphere, riding frequently with the Bangalore Hunt and at Ootacamund, and playing tennis whenever he could make the time. And he vastly enjoyed the scenery and natural history that he encountered. A letter written to Joyce from Government House at Ootacamund, on 18 May 1938, gives a particularly vivid account of the delight this caused him, and I make no apology for quoting from it at length.

> '*I have just arrived from Malappuram* [on the Malabar Coast] – *8000 feet climb since 10 a.m., and really I think one of the most sensational days I ever had in my life … We started from the absolute limit of tropical luxuriance, the most notable feature being the Areca Nut palm with a head like a toddy palm, but with the most incredibly long thin and pliant stem I ever dreamt of. I never saw so graceful a thing.*

> '*After 10 or 15 miles we entered a narrow belt of dry … jungle mostly teak, and then, starting to climb, re-entered the most magnificent tropical jungle where after another 10 miles or so we climbed the western ghats by a most spectacular road.*

'I drove the car with the steering wheel spinning in my hand like a teetotum – all in top or second – flying up this narrow winding road without the temperature of the car rising one degree. I never drove a car like it before. The air is exceptionally humid today and the blues of the distances and shadows coupled with the green of the jungles – with great masses of cumulus clouds covering the tops – made the views something to remember.

'After some 45 miles . . . I handed over to Lance [his ADC] and sat back to enjoy myself. We started from a filling station where I dried off my saturated back in the sun and breeze, surrounded by about a dozen bulbuls all singing most sweetly.

'We then climbed about one and a half hours through a, to me, entirely new vegetation, tea, coffee, blue gum, holm oak, another peculiar oak, and finally conifers of types quite unfamiliar – besides 1000 other queer things and many beautiful ones – great golden St John's Wort like the English garden one and some fine flowering trees.

'At 1 p.m. at say 7000 feet we lunched by a trout stream running through a grassy valley more like an ornamental park in Wales or Scotland than anything else I can think of. I got out of the car into a meadow full of gentians! – I enclose some samples – also leontopodium (is this right? – edelweiss family), lousewort, daisies, spiraeia globularia, and a number of semi familiar little alpine or English type things.

'By the way of course I should say that at every turn of the road the air had been getting cooler and fresher, and by now

I was glad of the coat of my flannel suit. There were heavy showers on the hills around which we just missed.

'We then motored on here, first over this curious plateau which one has heard so much about – a wonderful country unlike anything I ever saw – mostly green grassy downs with all the little valleys and watercourses full of rather stunted forest … and with a certain amount, not much, of scattered lichen-covered grey rocks lying about on the surface, but no rocky summits to any of the hills that I could see. Roads mostly lined with gums of various sorts – some very beautiful – and holm oaks (at least I think so).

'After 10 or 12 miles over this really unique plateau all at 7000 to 8000 feet, one enters Ooty, which is too different from any other place I have met in India to make any comparisons. It reminded me more of Ziarat than of any of the regular hill stations, as it is in a sort of basin, but of course 10 times as big and with quite a different vegetation.

'At 3 p.m., we entered Government House grounds – another sensation – gardens of purely English flowers of every conceivable kind all in full flower and all blooming away together – vast extent – and lawns with clover, daisies, dandelions etc. just like England. Finally, a palace, where I now write in a <u>suite</u> (4 rooms of sorts) with a wood fire! One must have spent some days on the Malabar coast to appreciate this. Their excellencies are at the races so I am going to have tea in peace and get out for a walk with my glasses [binoculars] before they come back.'

These glimpses of an earthly paradise were an occasional relief from the tedium of his official duties. But life was made much more bearable by the arrival of Joyce, Nannie and the three children in October, having sailed to Bombay in the *Viceroy of India*. The voyage, which had been planned for some months, was in danger of being called off, almost up to the day of sailing by the Munich crisis, which came to a head at just that time. The securing of a further, temporary as it turned out, period of peace lifted the shadow of last-minute cancellation. They settled into Flagstaff House, the bungalow that was his official residence in Bangalore, which he had painstakingly furnished for their arrival. By present-day standards the accommodation was not luxurious. Air conditioning was of course still in the remote future, but rather surprisingly the house did not even have ceiling fans. Bangalore, despite being at an altitude of some 3,000 feet above sea level, had sweateringly hot and humid seasons when, with bedroom windows wide open at night, mosquito nets were essential.

Reunited with his family, Teddy was able to relax and enjoy his life more than in the six months just past. Bill and I used to look forward eagerly every day to his return from work, when he would settle down and tell us the latest instalment of the long-running saga of 'Hill-and-Bugh-land', peopled by giants and ogres that he illustrated on the spot in terrifying detail. Dick, who had been taken out of school for a term, to enable the whole family to be together in one place, and to spend more time with his father, stayed in Bangalore until January 1939. He then left to resume his studies at West Downs in Winchester, and to prepare himself for the entrance exam to Winchester College.

An anecdote told to him by Joyce much later throws some light on Teddy's habit of bottling up his emotions. After he had gruffly bidden farewell to Dick as he departed for Bombay and the sea voyage, Teddy went into the garden of Flagstaff House the same evening and burst into tears. He was perhaps anticipating a separation from Dick of a year or so. He could not, of course, know then that the fortunes of war, interrupting the freedom of travel between England and India, would mean complete separation from Dick for a period of over two years, and in effect, bar two short interludes, for five years. He undoubtedly felt strong affection for his children, but, due in part to his upbringing, he found it easier to express it in ways such as this, and through his letter writing, than by physical contact or extravagant words when in their presence. How truly had he written to his fiancée in 1925, 'It seems we are neither of us much given to wearing our hearts on our sleeves.'

Dick had thoroughly enjoyed his exotic three-month sabbatical, and did not suffer from missing a term's schooling, since in June 1939 he sat for, and was awarded, a scholarship to Winchester College, a considerable academic achievement. He started his education at Winchester in September.

Meanwhile the attractions of Teddy's job did not increase, and as the world moved inexorably towards war in the first half of 1939, his frustration grew at being so remote from the cauldron where political and military preparations for a European war were in full swing. During this tense period, in June, news arrived that he had been awarded the CB – Companion of the Order of the Bath – in the King's Birthday Honours list. This honour is given, in its military division, as a reward for senior officers with a record of outstanding service in positions of command responsibility. The citation for his award no longer exists, but, given the short time that had elapsed since his assumption of the Bangalore job, there seems little doubt that his performance as BGS Aldershot Command was the main reason for it. Investiture at Buckingham Palace being impractical, he was ceremonially invested with the insignia by the Governor of the Madras Presidency, Lord Erskine, in December that year. Rather surprisingly, the investiture took place not in Madras, Lord Erskine's official seat, but in Bangalore, at Flagstaff House.

On 3 September war was declared against Germany. I remember, at the age of three, my father coming into the room on his return from the office to announce this news to his family. It meant very little to me. There was no immediate impact on his working life as commander Madras District, even though the political tension in the district, a stronghold of the Congress Party which opposed India's involvement in the war, must have risen markedly.

In May of the following year, however, he was transferred, after just over two years in Bangalore, to return to Quetta and assume command of the Western Independent District, a command also carrying the rank of major general, but reporting direct to the high command in Delhi. On May 19th the Norton family arrived in Quetta and occupied the official residence of the commander, Orchard House on the outskirts of the town. Orchard House was a two-storey building set in rather larger grounds than Flagstaff House and, with its fine view across the plain to a range of small mountains on the horizon, made a contrast to the more enclosed surroundings of their former home. They settled in with every expectation of a stay of some years, little guessing that, exactly two months after their arrival, a totally unexpected turn of events would split the family, and pitch Teddy into a new and unprecedented experience.

Teddy with Dick, his eldest child (right), and his father-in-law, William Pasteur.

Arriving in Hong Kong to take up his post, the acting governor is careful to avoid wearing his military uniform.

6

ACTING GOVERNOR OF HONG KONG

HONG KONG – THE BACKGROUND

In July 1940, Teddy was abruptly hustled away from his new command in Quetta and sent to Hong Kong, to become acting governor of the colony during the absence on medical leave of the governor, Sir Geoffry Northcote. He went unaccompanied by his family, who remained in India throughout his appointment. This is how it all came about.

With the threat of expansion by imperial Japan looming at its door-step, the defence of Hong Kong against a possible Japanese attack had been debated at length by the British Government and the chiefs of staff, and, to a lesser extent, by the Government of Hong Kong, in the years preceding the outbreak of war with Germany. Studies and 'appre-ciations' were carried out in 1937 and 1938, and the conclusion reached in a cabinet paper was that 'Hong Kong is not a vital interest … In the event of war, Hong Kong must be regarded as an outpost and held as long as possible', but 'we should resist the inevitable strong pressure to reinforce Hong Kong, and we should certainly be unable to relieve it.' When the war cabinet was formed, Winston Churchill emphatically backed this view – that Hong Kong was a strategic embarrassment, in effect impossible to defend against a determined Japanese invasion and therefore doomed to be overrun, and that the temptation to deploy major resources in its defence must be absolutely resisted.

Of course, this conclusion was not made public, either in England or in Hong Kong. Indeed the conclusion was not unanimous. Throughout the years 1937–1941 the debate rumbled on. Some participants argued that Hong Kong should be resourced with enough military power to fight off an invasion. Others, initially at least, argued that there would be no Japanese threat, since Britain enjoyed good diplomatic relations with Japan, and the recent history was one of military co-operation. Britain had helped the Japanese to build up their navy, the foundation of Japan's victory over Russia in their 1904–1905 war. How could they be other than friendly? This view seems to have prevailed in the colonial office, the department responsible for the civil administration in Hong Kong and for the appointment of its governors. It was certainly held widely by the resident expatriate, mainly British, population of Hong Kong, both businessmen and officials, who protested that any talk of the threat of invasion was alarmist, and could unnecessarily provoke Japan. It was best to continue quietly with business as usual, in the belief that if you did not upset them the Japanese would direct their hostility elsewhere.

This was the climate of opinion that Teddy would walk into on his arrival in the colony. The governor and his officials, however, being in the know about London's policy thinking, could not share this complacent attitude, and so a secondary issue, that of the amount of 'passive defences' (in effect, air raid precautions or 'ARP') that should be prepared in case of invasion, also became the subject of back-and-forth debate. The quietists, including most of the Hong Kong establishment and, it would appear, Northcote, took the view that any serious investment in air raid shelters was either too impractical or too expensive or both, and it was wiser to keep heads down and hope for the best. As late as October 1940, Northcote, who had by then been back in England on medical leave for five months, wrote in a note to the war cabinet that,

> 'the approved ARP policy is that residents should, as far as possible, stay in their houses, trenches being dug in the streets and the few open places for those caught out of doors. Most of the streets … are too narrow for trench-digging, however.'

The opponents of this do-nothing policy were aghast at its inadequacy, and pressed for a vigorous campaign of tunnelling into the granite hillsides that abound in Hong Kong and immediately surround the urban centres, to provide safe shelters from bombing for large numbers of the population. One of them wrote, in rather emotive language,

> 'this would perhaps do something to mitigate what otherwise promises to be one of the bloodiest holocausts in history, if and when Japanese bombing starts in earnest. The alternative is the prospect of thousands of stinking corpses and a fear-maddened people spilling out over the hillsides or sculling over the waters, thus impeding the defences.'

This then was a second, though not the last, controversy into which Teddy would walk on his arrival in Hong Kong. The heat had been turned up on these two issues – the appropriate level of effort to repel a Japanese invasion, and the precautions against bombing raids – by events shortly before his arrival. In May 1940, Northcote, who suffered from a recurrent heart condition, had a serious episode and, at the insistence of his doctors, was invalided out and shipped back to London for specialist treatment. His place was taken, on an acting basis, by Norman Smith, the colonial secretary in Hong Kong, in other words the most senior official under the governor, and the natural appointee to act in these circumstances. Then in June, with the Japanese invasion of China largely complete, Japanese forces appeared suddenly, and in strength, on the northern border of the colony with mainland China. For a short while it appeared highly likely that they were preparing to invade. Indeed, Japanese official papers that came to light after the war show that this was being seriously considered at the time. Alarm bells rang loudly in London and in Government House in Hong Kong, and the debates about how best to prepare for an imminent attack erupted with renewed vigour – though not, it would appear, among the resident expatriates, who remained blithely confident that all would be well.

One result of this flurry was that the government in Hong Kong, spurred on by directives from the Colonial Office in London, enacted in late June, with little warning, a compulsory evacuation order. This stated that all wives and children of 'European' families living in Hong Kong must be evacuated without delay as a safety precaution. They were to go initially by sea to the Philippines and from there to Australia, where arrangements would be made for their accommodation for as long as was necessary. Exemptions would be granted to women who could show that they were required for essential duties in the colony. American and some continental European nationals were covered by a similar instruction, given at a slightly later date by their own governments.

Right from the start, the order was highly controversial, and this caused a fury of complications to its administrators. Teddy would write, within a week of his arrival, of having to '*stand up to the bitterest hostility to the government*' in this matter. The difficulties were several. The expatriate population had not been prepared for the order and, as explained, had little belief in the need for it. There were difficulties over definitions. What was or was not a 'European' family? What about mixed-race families? There was an unfortunate use of the word 'pure' in attempting an exact ethnic definition, which not surprisingly caused deep offence. What were the 'essential duties' that justified exemption? It was observed that Hong Kong suddenly got a big increase in the number of nurses and government typists. The arrangements for financial support for the separated families were vague, and when they were eventually clarified, were almost immediately repealed, indeed to add insult to injury there was talk of repayments being demanded.

To make matters worse, the evacuation order was blatantly flouted by a fair number of government employees, including some very senior ones indeed, and this naturally added to the indignation felt by many. A more serious objection was that the order took care of a small number of expatriate families, but left the very large Chinese majority unprovided-for. The Chinese community leaders, meanwhile, simply advised their nationals to make their own arrangements for departure, at their own cost. All in all, it was an unfortunate piece of regulation, poorly administered, and one that would give Teddy a great deal of difficulty from the start.

Against this background, the difference of opinion was sharpening between those who took the threat of Japanese invasion seriously and those who did not. The chiefs of the British naval and military forces in the Hong Kong garrison teamed up to write to their superiors in London in early June, deploring the inadequate way that Norman Smith – who would be described by a later governor as 'that charming but exasperating fellow' – was addressing the urgent need for improved defence precautions, and begging for an acting governor with more military knowledge and grasp of the realities. This was put forward in cabinet by the secretary of state for war, and, after consultation with the secretary of state for the colonies, Teddy Norton's name was proposed to take up the position of acting governor, with Smith resuming his colonial secretary post. The reason for this choice can only be guessed, but presumably it was some combination of his perceived track record and aptitude for the task, and his relatively easy availability from a location not too far from Hong Kong. Be that as it may, the prime minister was persuaded of the merits of the idea, and the king's consent obtained. On 30 June, a royal commission was issued appointing Teddy to the post. He left Quetta on 19 July to proceed to Hong Kong.

It was clear that, with the controversy over the evacuation order raging, it would be absolutely inappropriate for his wife and family to accompany him. He resigned himself to another unaccompanied posting, remembering all too clearly how distressed he had been by separation in the early months of his stay in Bangalore, and arranged for Joyce and the family to take temporary accommodation in Ziarat. They later moved to Bombay, then Bangalore, then Ootacamund. The duration of his appointment in Hong Kong was by definition open-ended, since his task was to stay there until Northcote was sufficiently recovered to resume his governorship. He seems to have expected, at the start, that Northcote would be fit to return before the end of the year, an expectation certainly encouraged by Northcote himself, who was keen to return as soon as he could persuade the doctors to sign him fit.

Of course, the most unusual aspect of the appointment was that it placed a serving soldier, with no previous experience of colonial administration, in a post almost always occupied by a civilian incumbent from the colonial service. The records say that Hong Kong had had one previous 'military governor', Sir Frederick Lugard in 1910–1912, but Lugard at the time of his appointment was no longer a serving soldier, and already had experience of colonial administration, so the parallel is not close.

There was some nervousness in London as to how the appointment would be received by the population in Hong Kong, both expatriate and Chinese. The official announcements studiously avoided the term 'military governor'. But inevitably it was talked about in Hong Kong in those terms, and rumours were afoot that the incoming governor would be a martinet whose role would be to 'crack the whip' and introduce more discipline into Hong Kong society. Teddy was advised to downplay his military background, at least in his public appearances, and he was careful to arrive in the colony wearing civilian clothes, and to wear uniform only when engaged in military duties. (The press were not fooled; the *China Mail* reported his arrival with the headline 'Military Governor Lands in Civilian Clothes'.) Technically he held two appointments. One was as acting governor. Strictly speaking, the formal title was 'officer administering the government', but he was known locally both as the OAG and as the acting governor. The other was as commander-in-chief of British forces in Hong Kong, and for this he was given the acting rank of lieutenant general. This was so that he could outrank the senior soldier already in post, Major General Grasett, whom he would shortly describe as a 'very good friend and wise counsellor'.

TAKING UP THE REINS

For the first time in his life, he travelled by air between postings, for part of the way. For the last leg from Singapore, where he broke his journey to be briefed by his counterpart colonial governor, he took ship, and arrived in Hong Kong harbour on 6 August. He later showed me a recently published book – intended as a light-hearted travel guide for the first-time visitor – that he had bought before going to Hong Kong. The introduction to this book opened with the sentence:

'In the days of our grandfathers, sea travel to Hong Kong from

England could take anything up to six months, but today, thanks to the miracle of modern aviation, we can complete the same journey in six days!'

A striking reminder of the slowness of international travel, by today's standards, not so very long ago.

The topography and appearance of Hong Kong's landscape was, to him, both unfamiliar and attractive. The city was built on an island, separated from the Chinese mainland by a narrow strip of sea which sheltered the colony's harbour. The island was one, and not the largest, of many that clustered offshore within the territory of Hong Kong. Onshore across the harbour lay the twin city of Kowloon, and behind it a swathe of largely rural terrain known at that time as the New Territories, all of which lay within the colonial boundaries. The international border, as it was in those days, with China stretched over a long distance, and was difficult either to patrol or to defend. Both Hong Kong Island and the New Territories are ruggedly mountainous and extensively forested. The territory has a sharply different climate between summer and winter (unlike Singapore, for instance), is afflicted by typhoons in the late summer and autumn period, and can be murky and very humid in summer, as well as suffering sharp spells of cold weather in winter, with occasional frosts in the higher regions of the New Territories. But after his climatic experiences in India, the weather did not strike Teddy as uncomfortable or challenging.

As when he had gone unaccompanied to Bangalore, he wrote a stream of letters to Joyce, which convey vividly his frame of mind during his time in Hong Kong. They are disappointingly sketchy about the politics of his job and about his official activities, since his letters, as those of any other resident of Hong Kong writing abroad, were liable to be, and in some cases were, opened by the official censor. This precluded him from touching on any sensitive matters of national security. In September, he wrote: '*Some day I shall have a lot to tell you on all these matters, but most of them are censorable, and even about those that aren't technically so, discretion forbids my writing my views fully in a letter liable to be opened.*'

And, it may be added at this point, detailed records of his time as acting governor are sparse, since the whole of the government archive in Hong Kong itself was destroyed at the time of the Japanese occupation. But he wrote frankly about his feelings, as for instance his antipathy to Singapore at the time he was passing through it – his dislike of large cities has been described before. '*I should hate to live here more than any other place I know, bar I suppose Madras, Bombay, Karachi and Calcutta. I wonder if I shall add Hong Kong to the list. I fear so.*' And he did.

He had been instructed, in his briefings for the post, that his first task was to form his own opinion of the defensibility of Hong Kong in the event of a determined attack, and to report it back to the war cabinet. It did not take him long to conclude that it was not defensible, and that Churchill had been right. But, even as he pondered this question, from the very start he also found himself confronted by '*four big questions which were sticking out a yard when I arrived here*' – the ARP question, the evacuation scheme ('*still miles from any satisfactory conclusion*', he wrote in late September), the creation of a stock of food reserves sufficient to support a siege, and the '*control of unchecked Chinese immigration*', meaning refugees from the Japanese campaigns in southern China. These four thorny issues occupied a great deal of his time and energies in the early months, and he tackled them in a firm and forthright fashion. A typical comment to Joyce in a letter of 26th September reads '*I had a very difficult Executive Council meeting in the morning*' (referring to the cabinet of Hong Kong) '*and an equally difficult Legislative Council meeting in p.m.*' (referring to Hong Kong's legislature), '*at both of which I was forcing through in the teeth of a lot of opposition and obstruction one of the essential defence measures connected with food reserves, that I am determined to get done without further delay.'*

He particularly applied himself to the drilling of tunnels into the granite hillsides to give the population protection from aerial bombardment – the step that the previous administration had deemed either unnecessary or *'too big and hopeless to tackle'*, in his words. First he sent a representative to inspect the tunnels at the Chinese city of Chungking, where extensive tunnelling into the city's hills had provided shelter for vast numbers from the air raids of the invading Japanese. Then, although Hong Kong's granite was a lot more problematic than the limestone at Chungking, he directed the work of tunnelling to be started.

In this he was actively encouraged by his Colonial Office superiors in London, who authorised the considerable expense involved (eight million Hong Kong dollars), but he cut corners in order to get the work done with the urgency that he was convinced was necessary. This network of air raid shelters was substantially completed within his tenure, and when the Japanese invasion duly came in December 1941, they were rapidly filled with civilians fleeing from the bombing, and unquestionably saved very many lives. An eyewitness at that time wrote that,

> 'the public shelters were filled to an unbelievable extent with Chinese who remained good-humoured and placid'

This is in complete contrast to the vision of 'fear-maddened people spilling out over the hillsides'.

He tackled with similar determination the shambles of the families' evacuation order – the matter of the 'dear departed', as he dubbed it. He insisted on completing the original plan for the compulsory evacuation of wives and families, widely evaded up till then. He had been particularly offended by the cynical evasion of the order by some senior government officials, among them the chief justice. This strict application of the rules earned him a great deal of unpopularity which, in some quarters, lingered on until his departure the following spring. *'By sending away all those who deliberately evaded the original order, I have stirred up a wasps' nest again'* he wrote on 21 October. But at the same time he advised London that he was dubious about the legal justification for making the evacuation compulsory, and once the initial disarray had been sorted out, the Government decreed in November an end to any further compulsory evacuations, though it continued to encourage and prepare for voluntary evacuation by families. It firmly resisted any attempt by those already evacuated to return, and this too earned it much unpopularity.

Thus his early months were a whirlwind of energetic activity addressing what he saw as 'an awful series of messes to clear up and nettles to grasp'. By mid-October, he was able to record, with some satisfaction, that *'Grasett was kind enough to say the other day that he reckoned I had achieved more in two months than had been done in the last two years. But though this is very kind ... I have only achieved a start.'* And in December, *'I always thought him* [Admiral Peters, the British naval supremo in Hong Kong, who was departing] *critical of my methods but he was very flattering and on saying goodbye said "Thank you for teaching me much wisdom."'*

Admiral Peters, some while later, called on the secretary of state for the colonies in London to convey his first-hand account of Teddy's impressive achievements as governor. Lord Lloyd is said to have remarked 'I wish I had known this earlier'.

Amid the turmoil, Teddy spared many thoughts for his father's time in Hong Kong over seventy years earlier, which he referred to in his radio address to the people of Hong Kong on the day after his arrival, causing considerable interest in the press. He wrote to Joyce on 9 August, three days after his arrival, that *'the whole place seems almost haunted by his memories for me … I am tracing his first wife's grave'*, and two weeks later *'I don't think I told you that one day this week I discovered the grave of my old Dad's first wife – "Edith wife of Edward Norton died 6 September 1872 aged 24 years", poor young thing.'*

His reservations about life in Hong Kong were not confined to the problems of his job, nor to the unwelcome demands of the social round, which, as in Madras District two years earlier, he found it impossible to warm to. He seems to have particularly resented the Hong Kongers' obsession with horse racing and race meetings. On 16 September *'I finish with lunch by invitation at the Races! Tomorrow – a proper way of spoiling a Saturday afternoon.'* It is a curious fact that, despite his keen horsemanship, he always nursed a strong antipathy to flat racing.

But as well as all this, he found the expatriate society of Hong Kong remarkably introverted and out of touch with the realities of the world outside. *'I have tumbled into a new world'*, he wrote at the end of August. *'We used to think in India that they didn't know there was a war on. This seems ten times more so here. That there should be any diminution in racing or social entertainment for instance simply means nothing to anyone here … The progress of these critical days in England never forms a topic of conversation, and I find less understanding of what is happening in Europe than anywhere I have been. I sometimes feel like Alice in Wonderland.'* Two weeks later: *'Hong Kong remains supremely aloof and uninterested. No one talks of these matters* [the German blitzkrieg, and the threatened invasion of England] *at meals or parties, and such as do haven't the vaguest idea of what it is all about. To me the whole atmosphere is quite incredible. I can't find anybody with whom to discuss these things intelligently, and seem shut in on myself.'*

Against this background, his efforts to create adequate civil defences continued to attract opposition. In early October he wrote *'I am certainly having some very difficult problems to tackle, and sometimes feel as if I am fighting a lone battle against endless obstruction and opposition … It is curious that with the situation as it is* [referring to the increased threats of Japanese aggression – Japan had entered into a formal pact with the Axis powers in September, clearly signalling its unfriendly intentions towards Britain] *I have to fight practically a lone hand here to get on with our defensive preparations, by which I mean such of them as are not the province of the fighting services. Their preparations have all been complete for months, as ours might have been.'*

There were a few compensations for this disenchantment, and sense of struggle, with the expatriate establishment. He played such sport as he found time for, birdwatched with local experts, and could occasionally relax in the hunting field, with the local drag hunt. He enjoyed Mountain Lodge, the Governor's higher-altitude summer residence in the mountainous spine of Hong Kong Island, both for its pleasanter climate than the heat and humidity of the official residence and offices below, and also for its 360-degree views, which he described as some of the most sensational he had ever come across. From this eyrie, he spent his few leisure hours walking in the rough wooded terrain of the mountains, sometimes alone and sometimes with Grasett or Peters. As for social interactions, he found relief from the European community in meeting the small Indian resident community, with whom he felt instinctively at ease, and who were impressed with his fluency in Hindustani and other Indian dialects.

Equally, he enjoyed getting to know the large Chinese majority in the colony, a race with which he had had little or no contact until now. He seems to have struck up a good rapport with them. In a press photograph of him standing head and shoulders above a group of Chinese notables, a waggish columnist described him as 'The Acting Gulliver of Hong Kong'. He certainly sympathised with their unenviable situation, treated generally as second-class citizens, and under constant pressure from the dreaded threat of Japanese invasion, which had already subjugated the closely related Chinese populations in the southern provinces. At this time, the Chinese population of the colony, which until the most recent years had been fairly stable at around one million, had swollen to about two million through the more or less uncontrolled influx of refugees from the Japanese advance in the south. Many of these immigrants were illegal, and the administrative problems they caused were among his headaches throughout his tenure.

His attitude to the services for the Chinese majority population is reflected in a letter written shortly after his arrival, speaking of the contrast between '*the big general hospital*' (mainly, if not exclusively, for European use),

> '*a perfect example of modern efficiency, and the big Chinese general hospital, the most dreadful thing I ever saw, entirely due to overcrowded population thanks to the Sino-Jap war, and to lack of funds – a real scandal for so rich a colony.*'

Later, in December, he wrote of the same hospital,

> '*Next Friday I am giving myself a treat. You remember the poor little tubercular children immobilised in frightful positions. I described them to you at one of the hospitals. Well, I am going to give them all a present apiece – a toy of some sort which they themselves have chosen and which they can play with in their restricted positions. In addition, I am providing a reserve dump of plasticine, wool, drawing books, picture books, pencils etc., so that the effect may not be too transient. I have been most nobly assisted in organising this*

by Mrs M.K. Lo, wife of one of my Chinese members of Council, so she and I are going together to have the pleasure of seeing the toys whacked out.'

The records are tantalisingly silent on the contacts between the Hong Kong government and the Japanese forces in South China. One of Teddy's letters refers very briefly to a formal contact he had with the Japanese authorities in Canton (now Guangzhou), the major city at the head of the Pearl River delta, not far from Hong Kong, *'over the restrictions on traffic by river with Canton which has been allowed to sizzle for months and which I think I must clear up, and may lead to considerable difficulties.'*

He also refers to giving interviews to Japanese journalists. There was, not surprisingly, a Japanese resident community in Hong Kong. It is generally accepted that Japanese espionage and intelligence about the British in Hong Kong was vastly superior to British intelligence about Japan's intentions. A well-known story relates how a Mr Yamashita, a Japanese barber at the Hong Kong Hotel, who regularly cut the hair of British serving officers and government officials – he is said to have cut the hair of the governor – would engage in conversation with his customers about shipping movements and the like, or simply listen silently to indiscreet conversations, and for months, maybe years, was a fertile source of intelligence reports to Japan. The fact that the Japanese regarded British military capabilities with contempt was known to the War Office but not, apparently, to the intelligentsia and decision-makers in Hong Kong.

By the middle of autumn, Teddy had put his stamp firmly on the issues that confronted him on his arrival, and, in the case of the air raid shelters and the food reserves, had had his way and embarked on the execution phase of his solutions. Other thorny issues continued to exercise him, but he was probably able to spend more time on the routine work of the governor, which he had concluded '*ought not to be very heavy*'. Meanwhile, his letters to his family bear frequent evidence of how acutely he missed them, and in particular his two younger sons, aged seven and four, who were passing through a stage in their development that he bitterly regretted missing. '*Give my best love to my little nippers*', he wrote in October, '*and try to make them recognise their dad when they do see him.*' And, rather sadly, in another letter in the same month, '*in the case of the little chaps, every month of their rapid growth is a month of happiness lost for ever.*'

This distress at separation from his nearest and dearest compounded his overall dislike of his assignment, and his doubts about what it would do to his career prospects. Before his arrival, he wrote from Singapore to Joyce of his '*doubt as to what my new job is going to be like. The nearer I get to it and the more I hear, the less I feel that it is going to be any use to me, while at the worst one may be in for every sort of anxiety and perhaps humiliation … Well, I suppose we've earned these sad times by too much happiness in the past.*' Experience quickly confirmed that '*I certainly haven't tumbled into an easy job*', and, in the light of the frustrations he felt at the lack of kindred spirits, '*as it is, I long to be back at my own job.*' But later, in a different mood, he complained at the prospect, after being relieved by Northcote's return from sick leave, of '*being once again relegated to some backwater*'. All in all, one might conclude that this was the least enjoyable to him personally of any appointment in his entire career, though it must be said that he was sometimes prone to adopt, in speech or correspondence, an exaggeratedly pessimistic tone. This was particularly in evidence when he got together with his brother Jack. Joyce referred to it as 'the Norton gloom', which she contrasted with the more light-hearted approach to life of her own Pasteur clan.

THE TENURE ENTERS A NEW PHASE

By late October, the initial furore from the backlog of contentious issues was dying down, and his life as acting governor settled into a more regular pattern. His letters at this time give a glimpse of the weekly routine of a governor. Mondays, and Tuesday and Thursday mornings, were spent dealing with paperwork generated by the government machine. Tuesday afternoons were for weekly meetings on defence, Chinese affairs and with the business community leaders. Wednesday mornings were given over to the Executive Council meeting – *'facing some big and controversial problem every time which takes all my tact and determination to get through – one finishes these meetings sometimes feeling quite battered'*. Every second Thursday afternoon was a Legislative Council meeting. Fridays were devoted to a War Council dealing with defence matters, both military and civil, followed by a tour of some part of the defences. Other afternoons were used for ARP inspections and visits to 'police, fire brigade, hospitals and refugee camps etc. etc.' Finally, regular business lunches twice a week and dinner parties for ten or more twice a week, *'invariably boring to the last degree and sometimes even more difficult with completely inarticulate Chinese ladies to take in.'*

For exercise, he was able to fit in a game of tennis a week, and took a walk of half an hour to an hour every day before breakfast at 8.15 a.m. But almost every corner of his spare time was taken up with the demands of incoming paperwork. *'An orderly comes into my study periodically bringing a bag something like a suitcase full of papers and files. After I have spent say 3 hours on interviews etc. ... this amounts to as many as 4 bags all full of papers of which one third are marked "urgent" and half of those "very urgent" ... Every hour I take outdoors looking at this that or the other in the way of business exacts its penalty and produces its pile of bags. It's like Sisyphus' task.'* He was critical of the management of workflow in the office, and wrote on 12 December *'If I were to stay here I should try to organise things to reduce much of this routine work.'*

With the exception of the families evacuation row, which rumbled on as bitterly as ever throughout his time as acting governor, he had by December broken the back of all the major tasks that confronted him on arrival. His letter to Joyce of 10 December observes '*I have really done what I came here for. There are a few loose ends to tidy up but everything important is now in train.*' The tunnelling, of course, was not complete, but the battles to overcome the inertia and get the work under way had been won. By the time he left the colony, he estimated that 100,000 people could be accommodated in these shelters, and a further 500,000–600,000 taken care of in safe dispersal areas; and the work of tunnelling continued after his departure.

As the months of his tenure ticked away, two additional concerns distracted him: the doubts and frequent changes of plan as to when Northcote would resume his office, and the doubts and frequent changes of plan as to what his own next appointment would then be.

The sequence began with a firm indication that Northcote would arrive back in Hong Kong in December, so firm that he wrote to Joyce in November of '*the certainty of Sir G. Northcote's return*' in mid-December. At this stage, he had been obliged to go into print forcefully objecting to a plan for Lady Northcote to accompany her returning husband. His objection carried weight, and Northcote eventually returned unaccompanied. As the weeks and months ticked by, the planned date of his return continually receded, to January, then to February, then to March, and Teddy found he was getting his information from newspaper reports and rumours. The Colonial Office was, in this matter at least, notably poor at either clear or prompt communication. Eventually, after a protracted sea voyage round the Cape, the returning governor landed in Hong Kong on 17 March 1941, and resumed his post forthwith.

In parallel with this, and believing at all times that his tenure might have only a month still to run, Teddy engaged in a lengthy campaign of correspondence to discover where his next career posting as a soldier would take him, and what would happen to his family. Only in the event of his returning to India could he be sure that he would be reunited with them. The War Office, with which he could only correspond via the Colonial Office, matched the latter in uncommunicativeness, merely telling him that he could expect to revert to the rank of major general when relieved of his appointment.

He seems to have believed in November that he would indeed be posted back to India, but by December he was writing that '*the more I think of it the less probability do I see of being employed in India.*' The likeliest alternative was that he would be summoned back to England, and this posed two unattractive scenarios. One was that he might sail back via the Indian Ocean and the Cape, in which case it might be possible to snatch a hasty reunion for a few days with his family in Singapore or Colombo ('*I can get there in four days by air*') before leaving them to make their way back to India, perhaps for the rest of the war. The other, that he might be instructed to travel eastwards across the Pacific and through the USA, in which case he would not even achieve that brief reunion. Either way, he assumed that they ought not to accompany him to England because of the submarine hazards to merchant shipping in the Atlantic, and in any case it was unclear whether the army would pay for their passages. On this last point, the War Office finally vouchsafed its idea of clarification at the end of February, by wiring him that it had 'not yet decided general principles for families whose heads are in Middle East or China. Reply to your cable will be sent when general decision made.' It never was.

It is not worth following the twists and turns of this correspondence. He doggedly debated with Joyce a series of options for them to enjoy a brief meeting somewhere in the Indian Ocean before he was dispatched back to England, and agonised over the possibility that even that might not be achieved, and they would be separated for a matter of years. On 31 January the War Office at last directed that he should on relinquishing the governorship 'return UK earliest available opportunity.' After a month of further pleas for clarity about the route and the cost of family passages, he received another cable on 28 February, 'You should await further orders before embarking for UK'. As he commented, *this leaves me completely guessing.'* In the end, he departed Hong Kong on 21 March to sail to Singapore, where he had secured permission for Joyce to join him from South India for a few days, before continuing the voyage back to England. Once there, he would be informed of his next assignment.

In the lead-up to this finale, the last month of his time in Hong Kong was marred by an unpleasant and potentially serious accident.

On 19 February he wrote to Joyce describing how on that day, while reviewing the whole range of the colony's defence problems, which he believed he had settled satisfactorily, he discovered that in one respect, *'and a vital one, I have been let down all along the line. Nothing was ready and the situation was chaotic … I am bitterly disappointed and feel a very heavy sense of responsibility, and instead of having a light heart and a clear conscience … I am up to my eyes in strenuous endeavours to clear up the mess.'* Censorship prevented him from identifying the issue that caused him this outburst of self-criticism, and it was overtaken by an episode that same evening.

Out for one of his strolls on the mountainside with General Grasett, as they were walking along the edge of a deep, concrete-lined open storm drain after heavy rain, Teddy slipped and fell, head first, a drop of eight feet into the concrete bottom of the drain and into several inches of stagnant water. Concussed and unconscious, and with his head and mouth underwater, he could well have drowned had it not been for the resourcefulness of Grasett, who was able to pick him up and shepherd him back to a road where transport could be found to take him home.

Although the overt injuries were confined to the after-effects of severe concussion and multiple heavy bruising, including a 'contused lung with pneumonic shadowing', his general health was set back considerably by this accident. He was spitting or coughing blood for over a week, and two weeks after the accident, having resumed full-time duties, was obliged to retire to bed again – less than two weeks before his final departure from Hong Kong. There is little doubt that he was not fully recovered by the time he left, and Joyce recalled that he was subdued and a shadow of his normal self when they met again in Singapore. His old friend Howard Somervell, a doctor himself, thought that the effect of the accident was to 'age him greatly', but this may have been an exaggeration.

This misfortune precluded his making much further impact on the remaining problems of the colony in the last few weeks of his stay. The official tributes paid to him in the Legislative Council on the eve of his departure, and the leading article the following day in the *South China Morning Post*, Hong Kong's leading broadsheet, make interesting reading. They leave the impression that the tributes of the British members of the council were somewhat guarded. Certainly they were less enthusiastic than the words of the leading Chinese Council member, who spoke with real warmth about the acting governor's impact on the colony, and how he had dealt with the concerns of the Chinese community.

An extract may give a flavour of this speech:

'I should like to record the gratitude of the Chinese members of the council for the way in which he took us into his confidence on numerous questions with which he had to deal, and the sympathetic manner in which he received representations we felt it our duty to make, as representatives of the Chinese. I venture to think that the number of functions which Lieutenant-General Norton attended during the short period of his administration must constitute a record. It is a matter of amazement to many of us how he could have found time to study and master so many different and difficult problems, and at the same time to get to know so many individuals in the Colony. He made his inspections frequently at hours when the rest of the Colony was still in bed, and it can be truly said that he never spared himself.'

The leading article, in more forthright style, sets out what are in its view not just the pluses but also the principal minus of the acting governor's tenure. After paying graceful tributes to his virtues and achievements, it weighs in on the running sore of the evacuation problem, describing it as 'the one important issue on which dissatisfaction remains acute.' But perhaps, it concludes, 'the orders came from the Imperial Government, and the Acting Governor's adamant attitude was official obedience.' The bruised feelings of certain senior government servants are thinly disguised!

An alternative judgement came from Brigadier French, a fellow passenger on the ship in which Teddy sailed on his departure from Hong Kong, in a letter to an acquaintance of Teddy's brother Jack – who described it as 'not bad for an unsolicited testimonial from a cynic!'

'When I got to Hong Kong I found your friend Norton there as acting governor. He is now on this ship on his way home. He has been a crashing success at HK. Everyone high and low, civil and military, European and Chinese have the greatest admiration for him and for his work during the seven months

he has been in HK. Personally I think him one of the nicest
and finest fellows I have ever met, and it has been a real
pleasure to get to know him.'

Before leaving Hong Kong, it is worth recalling what happened in the
remaining months of 1941. Sir Geoffry Northcote resumed the reins of
the governorship, but unfortunately his medical condition reared its
head again, and in September he was once more sent home for medical
care, and this time gave up his post for good. He was succeeded by
another Colonial Office appointee, Sir Mark Young.

Meanwhile, during the spring and summer of 1941, the policy of
minimal preparation for the defence of Hong Kong was being urgently
reviewed once again in London. As late as January, Churchill had still
been asserting in print his belief that no further military resources
should be put into Hong Kong:

'If Japan goes to war with us, there is not the slightest chance
of holding Hong Kong or relieving it. It is most unwise to
increase the loss we shall suffer there. Instead of increasing
the garrison it ought to be reduced'.

But he too in the end changed his mind, and the result of the review
was a volte-face in policy. Extra troops were scrambled into Hong Kong
to reinforce the garrison in the late summer and autumn.

It was too late. As part of its spectacular eruption into combatant
status in the Pacific and the Far East in December, Japan launched
an attack on Hong Kong in the middle of the month. After a short,
one-sided campaign involving widespread aerial bombing, the colony
fell on Christmas Day 1941 and the Japanese occupied it. Sir Mark
Young, in common with most of the British population, was interned

at Stanley on the island for the duration of the war, and only emerged in 1945, to resume his interrupted governorship.

THE PATH TO RETIREMENT

Teddy and Joyce met in Singapore under the roof of the governor, Sir Shenton Thomas, for a final chance to discuss the family's immediate plans, and to say goodbye, before they went their separate ways, he to England and she back to India and the family. The prospect of separation for an unknown period, possibly years rather than months, stared them in the face. But while they were there, the War Office struck again. Teddy's orders to proceed to London were countermanded, and he was instructed to return at once to India. Their forward plans were torn up, and with great delight, no doubt, that the family would be reunited after all, but perhaps with a slight feeling of emotional anticlimax, they sailed for India. They landed at Negapatam in early April, went up-country to Ooty to collect Nannie and the boys, and all travelled north to Quetta where they arrived in May.

He had been sent back to his old job in Quetta, commanding Western Independent District, but the scope of the command had been enlarged, partly reflecting concerns about a possible German advance from southern Russia across Central Asia to invade India from that quarter. As a result, he was, contrary to what he had been told, allowed to keep his rank of lieutenant general, though still on an acting basis. So the Norton family settled again into Orchard House, which they had left just ten months ago, and into a similar routine, except that Joyce, who had trained as a stenographer while Teddy was in Hong Kong, took a job with the army HQ cipher office, and Bill started at a new school.

To backtrack for a moment: Dick, at the age of thirteen, had, to his mild astonishment, been put on a ship back to India after only one year at Winchester College, arriving in September 1940 after a voyage in convoy round the Cape. This decision had been taken by his parents, after much debate, at a time when the south of England was on invasion alert, and his father was uneasy at the prospect of having the family split in three far-flung locations. He attended a school briefly while in Ooty, but by April 1941 it was thought high time for him to resume more serious secondary education than was available in India. Returning to England, however, with submarine attacks on shipping in the Atlantic constantly in the news, was not an option.

His parents had discussed these matters at length in their exchange of letters the previous winter, and continued to do so in Ooty, with Dick also involved in the discussion. Given the absence of anything suitable in India, a boarding school in South Africa, St Andrew's College at Grahamstown, had been earmarked for him. So in May, while the rest of the family went to Quetta, Dick again took ship from Bombay to Durban, travelling alone aged fourteen, and restarted his much-interrupted schooling at Grahamstown. He would live in South Africa for the next two and a half years, during the first year of which he was separated from his family, and stayed with family friends or acquaintances during school holidays.

The next year in Quetta was relatively uneventful for the Norton family. For myself, aged nearly five when we arrived, the fragments of memory that stuck with me were sitting in the garden under an apricot tree, picking ripe apricots for breakfast; listening to jackals baying after dark, just beyond the garden fence; and being rushed downstairs and out of the house very early in the day because an earthquake had struck, the house was shaking, and the roof tank on top of the house was cracked and spilling water down the walls. This earthquake, in September 1941, was a minor affair compared to the disaster of 1935, but serious enough to conjure up dreadful memories of the dead buried under collapsing buildings only six years earlier. Fortunately much of the town had been reconstructed earthquake-proof, the damage was very minor, and there was no loss of life.

With his enlarged responsibilities, Teddy was pleasantly surprised at the variety and challenge of the work, despite the remoteness from the wartime theatres of operations, which was where he really wished to be. The job was busy and intensive and, inevitably, involved large amounts of travel around his district, and to Karachi and Delhi. Early on in this period he met General Sir Archibald Wavell on his arrival in India from Cairo to take up the post of commander-in-chief (he later became viceroy). The official line was that Wavell had become tired and needed a spell away from an active theatre of war, but Teddy commented that he did not appear tired in the least, and it was widely suspected that the real reason for Wavell's move was his clashes with Churchill.

Teddy's health, initially poor after the accident at Hong Kong, and compounded by one of his periodic bouts of malaria, improved steadily once the summer was over and the cold weather set in. He devoured the news about the progress of the war and took an intense, but academic, interest in the strategic decisions of the combatant parties. But the news of the fall of Hong Kong, and of Singapore in the following spring, caused him deep concern, since he knew well so many of the leading personalities involved, and many of the internees at both locations. A small consolation was a report that reached him from one of the few escapees from the siege of Hong Kong, who confirmed the immense value of the air raid shelters that had been his legacy, and the small number of civilian casualties that had resulted.

But his mix of enjoyment and frustration at this 'backwater' posting was short-lived, since in May 1942, only twelve months after his arrival in Quetta, fresh instructions again arrived from London. He was to relinquish his Western Independent District command and report in person to the War Office for further assignment. So once more the peripatetic family packed up their bags and began their travels. They took the train to Bombay, and in late May embarked on the SS *Windsor Castle* to sail across the Indian Ocean.

With Dick at school in Grahamstown, South Africa was a natural staging post on the journey back to England. The *Windsor Castle* did not make port at Durban, so they disembarked on 7 June at Cape Town, where Teddy planned to take a few weeks of the leave due to him. They found accommodation, and the debate between Teddy and Joyce as to whether she, and the family, should accompany him back to England, despite the threat to Atlantic shipping from German submarines, came to a head. He was adamant that he would not allow his family to run that risk, and that he must go ahead alone. She was furious at the prospect of a third period of marital separation, and used all her arguments to persuade him otherwise. But in the end he had his way. She later described it as the only serious row of their marriage.

So Joyce and the family were installed in a service flat in a hotel in Rondebosch, a suburb of Cape Town. She took, a few months later, a job at the cipher office in the British naval HQ in Cape Town, to supplement the family's finances while they were on their own in South Africa.[1]

Meanwhile, the two of them took the train journey across country to Grahamstown to visit Dick at St Andrew's College, staying there a week in the headmaster's house. They had been pleased with reports of the school and of Dick's progress that reached them while still in Quetta, and closer acquaintance evidently confirmed their approval, since Dick continued with his education there, and Bill was enrolled at the boarding prep school attached to the college, which he attended

1 She used to describe, and deplore, the very lax standards of security at her place of work.

from September. While my two older brothers shuttled back and forth between Cape Town and Grahamstown at the start and end of each term, I attended my first day school in Rondebosch.

Teddy's period of leave in South Africa came to an end, and in early July he set sail for England in the *Warwick Castle*, landing at Glasgow on 19 August. With no home of his own in England, he went to live with Jack and Madge at Greenhill, their Hampshire house. From there he commuted to London to attend the War Office, as directed, and await news of his next appointment. Up to this point, he had still hoped against hope that he could yet receive a final command appointment in an active theatre of operations. He certainly felt himself to be perfectly well equipped for this, both as to experience and skill, and as to vigour and fitness. But it was not to be. In October 1942, he was informed that he was being placed on the retired list with immediate effect, and was promptly given a Home Guard appointment as sector commander for the North Hampshire sector – not, as he had speculated in one of his gloomier letters from Hong Kong, as a Home Guard private.

At the point of retirement, he was finally given the honorary rank of lieutenant general, having been an acting lieutenant general for the previous two years. To be retired at the age of fifty-eight-and-a-half years was by no means unusual. Among senior serving officers, normal retirement age had been getting progressively lower for some years. Others of his rank had been retired at this age or even younger. He and Joyce had discussed the possibility of this happening when reviewing his likely next career step in Quetta, and it cannot have come as a complete surprise, though no doubt he had to swallow a feeling of disappointment. So ended the full-time part of a distinguished military career, which had started slowly, burst out into a phase of very high promise, later slowed its rate of ascent, and finally branched out into an unexpected direction before it reached its end.

Teddy (left) greets the C-in-C General Sir Archibald Wavell on his arrival at Quetta, 1941.

A formal portrait of Teddy in 1952.

7

RETIREMENT

PUTTING DOWN ROOTS IN HAMPSHIRE

Teddy's family remained in South Africa while the dangers of submarine attacks on shipping in the Atlantic continued. Joyce kept on at her job at the naval cipher office, Dick and Bill attended boarding school in Grahamstown, and Nannie looked after me while I attended my Rondebosch kindergarten. In September 1943, fourteen months after Teddy had left them to set sail for England, Joyce's father died at home at the age of eighty-six. Bereavement was the harder for her to bear not only from her great affection for him, but also from their enforced separation a hemisphere apart.

It was in fact in the same month that my parents agreed that the submarine menace had receded enough for the family to travel back to England. Joyce secured passages on an ocean liner that had been commandeered as a troopship, the *Strathaird*, and we set sail from Cape Town at the end of September.

I remember the voyage as a colourful experience for a seven-year-old. Although there were a fair number of paying passengers, the majority of those on board were British troops returning from overseas service. Two cabins were taken in which Joyce, Nannie and the two younger boys were cooped up for the six-week voyage, while Dick, not yet seventeen years old, was assigned a hammock slung in the junior officers' section. Our older cousin, Chris Norton, the younger son of Jack, was also on board, being a serving soldier at the time. The *Strathaird* formed part of a small, strange convoy of which the other members were a huge and aged battleship, the *Lorraine*, one of the French naval vessels that had been assimilated by the British when France was over-run by Germany, and which would shortly see active service as part of the British naval bombardment of occupied France; and three British Navy frigates as escorts to the ill-assorted pair. Part of the reason for the long drawn-out voyage time was the slow sailing speed of the *Lorraine*, whether from old age or from some crippling damage sustained in hostilities I am not clear. The little convoy limped up the west coast of Africa, staying mostly at sea but calling into port twice to provision, at Pointe-Noire in French Equatorial Africa and at Freetown in Sierra Leone. The safety of a sea voyage in the Atlantic was by no means a foregone conclusion. Regular lifeboat drills were held. On at least one occasion a suspected enemy warplane was spotted, and we were alerted to go to our lifeboat stations. It was, in any case, mandatory to carry life jackets with us at all times. Since there was a woeful shortage of chairs for the passengers, these were used by many as makeshift seats, both on deck and in the saloons.

During the days, a school of sorts was organised to occupy the younger children on the ship, and in the evenings Bill would entertain me by reading aloud the latest of the macabre stories that he had a talent for writing, entitled 'The Phantom Destroyer' and featuring, as far as I recall, a crew consisting entirely of skeletons. Ship's concerts and raffles were held, in an effort to simulate the conditions of peacetime cruising.

At Gibraltar, the *Strathaird* left the convoy and we stayed in port for a few days, after which we joined a much larger convoy of merchant shipping heading out of the Mediterranean to Britain. This involved sailing for half a day east from Gibraltar, and then doing a 180-degree turn to melt into the merchant shipping convoy after dark, all vessels sailing with the minimum of lights on a moonless night in virtual blackout – a romantic experience for a seven-year-old. Escorted by destroyers, this was a much faster-moving convoy, and, being nearer to the scene of hostilities, precautions against attack were taken more seriously than further south. There was a scare when a lurking U-boat had to be driven away with depth charges, but the convoy sustained no damage, and within a few days we were disembarking at Glasgow. As a child who had been a long way from Britain throughout the Second World War till now, it was a novelty to experience my first air raid sirens, heard from the train as we chugged southwards towards London.

So the family was reunited in November after its third period of separation, and put down roots, temporarily at least, in a rented house in Micheldever, a village north of Winchester, which Teddy had taken in preparation for our return, and which suited his North Hampshire Home Guard appointment. Although the war still had eighteen months to run until VE (Victory in Europe) day, village life in rural Hampshire had little of the atmosphere of a nation at war. But there were occasional exceptions. Through the middle months of 1944, traffic on the main roads near Micheldever was periodically interrupted to allow endless convoys of army vehicles to pass towards the coast, as part of the D-Day landings build-up, and Hampshire was designated as a 'Restricted Area' to prevent unwanted non-residents from entering it and observing the preparations. Then there was the blackout. All curtains had to be lined with blackout material, and no lights were supposed to show from any buildings at night. And once, a V-1 or 'doodlebug', one of the primitive first-generation long-distance missiles aimed by Germany at London and Southampton, having gone astray from its target, was heard ploughing through the skies overhead, and then hitting the ground with a loud explosion nearby. This so much dismayed an evacuee family from the East End of London, who had just arrived at our house precisely so as to escape the missile threat in the capital, that they packed their bags and returned home immediately. Otherwise, however, even in the midst of 'austerity' and the rigours of wartime rationing, life had a peaceable quality, and we never heard or saw any of the second-generation missiles, the faster and more dangerous V-2s that caused so much damage in London.

Teddy's Home Guard appointment lasted just under two years, until August 1944. He seldom spoke about it, probably not rating it highly as a military experience, though he undoubtedly performed it in his normal conscientious way. The Home Guard, by no means merely a Dad's Army, had an important role to play in guarding strongpoints during the D-Day build-up. During 1944, he was approached and offered the post of governor, South Australia, which became vacant in April of that year. This post appears to have been regularly occupied, at that period, by senior retired officers of the British armed forces, and the offer no doubt took account of his track record as acting governor of Hong Kong, though the duties would have been a lot more ceremonial. It also seems probable that it would have brought him the award of a knighthood. After consulting with Joyce, however, he declined the offer, partly from reluctance to uproot his family once more to a distant land, with all the accompanying problems of schooling for their sons, but also, I believe, because he estimated that accepting the post, far from being remuner-ative, would force him to supplement its salary from his own pocket.

His stepping down from his Home Guard post in August 1944 coincided with the disbanding of the Home Guard, and he was immediately appointed commandant of the Hampshire contingent of the Army Cadet Force (ACF), an appointment that lasted four years until August 1948. The ACF, a voluntary organisation, largely officered by schoolmasters in their spare time, aimed to give schoolboys a taste of military life coupled with adventurous experiences, as a possible precursor to their enlisting in the regular army. His role, as well as directing the county force in its day-to-day activities, involved a degree of financial administration and lobbying for funds from the central budget. In addition to these more or less active appointments, he held, from early 1942, just before his retirement, until 1949, the appointment of colonel commandant Royal Artillery, an honour of largely ceremonial significance given to gunner generals, normally after retirement.

In August 1944, his older sister Amy died of cancer, leaving her husband W (Alexander Wardrop) a widower. Shortly after this, and having spent a brief spell in the Home Guard, Dick decided to follow in his father's career footsteps as a regular soldier, and joined up as a gunner in April 1945, receiving a commission in August 1946; Teddy presided at his passing out parade from the Officer Cadet Training Unit at Deepcut. He would indeed follow in his father's footsteps closely, since much of the early part of his regular service was in various regiments of the Royal Horse Artillery. For two and a half years, from 1948 to 1950, he served with the King's Troop RHA, carrying out frequent ceremonial duties for the Crown.

In June 1945 the Nortons finally bought their own house in Hampshire, and settled in to what would be Teddy's last home. Morestead Grove was a four-bedroomed former rectory of early nineteenth century date in the tiny village of Morestead just south of Winchester, with a garden of about half an acre. The location was close to a small cluster of his immediate family. His two surviving siblings out of the original six, Jack and Gillie, both lived a short way south with their spouses, and so did W, who occupied a large country house with extensive wooded grounds and two live-in servants.

Of the three relatives, W was undoubtedly the most colourful. Although my own memories of him are of his declining years in the post-war era, when he suffered from very poor eyesight and was none too mobile, his fiery and unconventional personality had survived his retirement as a regular soldier, with the rank of general, in 1937. When the Home Guard was formed in 1940, he promptly joined up in the ranks as a private soldier. A photograph shows him standing stiffly to attention in his private's uniform, sporting a very military moustache and, incongruously, the monocle that he always wore. The platoon that he joined, like all Home Guard units at the start, had no weaponry supplied to it, but W provided it with an assortment of shotguns and other firearms from his own gunroom.[1]

On another occasion, when Teddy and W both had to attend a formal military ceremony in Winchester, W offered to give Teddy a lift. He arrived at Morestead Grove to collect him on his motorbike, and the two generals, in full ceremonial dress, roared off down the road to Winchester, with Teddy riding pillion.

To visit W's house near Upham for lunch was a sort of throwback experience. Even when entertaining only his brother-in-law's family, he liked strict formality over the lunch table. His housemaid Norman (her surname, of course) would enter the drawing room where we sat before the meal, properly attired in her black and white housemaid's uniform with cap and pinafore, and declaim, in her characteristically strangulated tones, 'Please Sir Alexander lunch is served'; while his Scottish cook Annie, who despised the formality, beavered away crossly

---

[1] It was not unusual for former army officers to join the Home Guard as rankers. One unit is said to have boasted eight retired generals in its non-commissioned ranks.

in the kitchen. But often there were other lunch guests, since W in his widower-hood seemed to attract a bevy of unattached, or sometimes attached, ladies of a certain age to come and keep him company. Joyce referred to these companions as 'W's harem'. As his eyesight deteriorated, he resorted to the typewriter for the writing of letters, and the results often included inadvertent, and sometimes hilarious, misprints.

After we had occupied Morestead Grove, Teddy was contacted by his former batman Charlie Hancock. He engaged him as gardener and general factotum, and his diminutive wife Olive as our cook, and set them up in a small bungalow cottage in the village. Hancock and his wife, together with Nannie Vockins who lived in, made up the rest of the household in addition to the family.

UNCOMPLICATED LIVING AT MORESTEAD

Life at Morestead Grove in these post-war years was a relatively simple affair. The rigours of wartime and post-war rationing meant that for several years the availability of food, clothing, fuel and, worst of all for us schoolboys, sweets was restricted. For instance, Teddy issued his two younger sons (Dick having left home) with a small block of butter each Monday, with instructions to make it last a full week – in which Bill was always successful, and I always failed by about Friday, much to my fury, and to Bill's amusement. We supplemented the food rationing by growing as much as possible in the fruit and vegetable section of the garden, and by keeping hens in a corner of the neighbouring farmer's field. The ration of coal, or coke, for the central heating, such as it was, and for the Aga cooker was collected by car from the nearest coal depot in Winchester, a task for which it was my job to help my father. Nor was the simplicity just a result of rationing. Electrical white goods for the home were almost non-existent. With no refrigerators, perishable food was kept cool, perfectly satisfactorily, in a larder with a small north-facing window. Clothes and linen were washed by hand, and dried with the help of an old-fashioned mangle, which I turned while my mother fed in the saturated sheets. Dishwashers had not been invented, so all meals were washed up by hand, Teddy allocating to each family member their role in the process.

There was no TV. The radio, or rather the 'wireless', was the source of news as well as entertainment. Every Christmas Day, we listened rather solemnly to the King's Christmas address to the nation, all standing to attention for the national anthem before and after the speech, for Teddy was a patriot and a monarchist, and could be a stickler for formalities. In more unbuttoned moods, he would listen with relish and with frequent bursts of laughter to the weekly instalments of *ITMA* starring Tommy Handley, his favourite comedian at the time. Entertainments in the evening after supper were often family games – poker or canasta, or simple pencil-and-paper games – or else attempting *The Times* crossword, the clues to which he would read out while the rest of us tried frantically to visualise the answers. I still recall the family's looks of amazement when I solved my first clue at an age when I was considered too young to take part in the collective effort. (I even remember the clue – 'Say what you like, it's our right – 7,2,6', and the solution, 'Freedom of speech'.) At other times, musical entertainment was provided by Joyce playing the piano, alone or in duet with one of her sons.

Since most of Morestead was not connected to any mains supplies, we made our own electricity with an old-fashioned generator known as a 'dynamo', located in the garage, which fed a bank of batteries. We got our water from a farm supply drawn from wells, cooked on a coal or coke oven, and warmed the rooms in winter with wood fires. When I was reckoned to be old enough to help with starting up the dynamo, Teddy took me into the garage to demonstrate the technique. Unfortunately machinery was not his forte, and as the massive flywheel gathered speed in the start-up procedure, he negligently allowed a metal-protected hand lamp on a long flex to be drawn into the flywheel mechanism. There was a deafening explosion and fragments of metal from the wheel flew about the garage. Very luckily, neither of us was hit. It was just as well that shortly after this episode the mains electricity supply arrived, and the dynamo could be decommissioned.

The passing months were punctuated by the visits of acquaintances from his earlier life. They included Field Marshall Alanbrooke, who regaled Teddy with a colourful account of the acute frustrations of working closely with Churchill during the war; from among his Everest friends, Howard Somervell, Ferdie Crawford and, in 1952, Eric Shipton, who at that stage was still expecting to lead the Everest expedition of 1953; and a good friend from his days in India, General Prem Singh Gyani.

Teddy was not wealthy. Once Bill asked him why the family couldn't take holidays abroad on the continent more often, and got the reply 'Sorry, old chap, can't afford it'. Instead, holidays were, for the most part, taken in Scotland, which exercised its magnetic attraction on both Teddy and Joyce, largely for the fishing that it offered, but also for the wild and mountainous country. Between 1946 and 1951, we went there in the summer five times, initially in the Southern Lowlands, but then for four years in the far north-western Highlands, twice to Loch Maree, and twice to Altnacealgach in Sutherland, a location recommended by Tom Longstaff, who lived nearby in a very remote house on the west coast. To get there, we took the overnight sleeper train from Euston, and were taught by Teddy that the first true taste of Scotland was the porridge served in the sleeper's restaurant car.

From the hotels where we stayed, he would take his sons out watercolour sketching with him, and both parents taught us to fish for brown trout in the hill lochs. Hillwalking was of course on the agenda. We also engaged in a favourite holiday occupation of earlier generations of the Nortons, the writing of a story. One chapter was contributed every two days by each member of the party, and read out aloud after supper. Teddy set the scene with the first chapter, usually creating a cast of thinly disguised characters from real life – a villainous 'Uncle Jock', Bill's and Hugh's housemasters (we had followed Dick to Winchester College) with comically distorted names, and so forth, sometimes illustrating them with his sharply drawn caricatures.

Joyce and Teddy celebrated their silver wedding anniversary in December 1950.

VISITING THE CHALET AND ARGENTINA

During this six-year period from 1946 to 1951, there was one exception to the rule of no family holidays abroad, a holiday at the Chalet. During the war, both the Chalet and the Collet Chalet, the Nortons' higher-altitude hut on the Plateau d'Anterne, had been commandeered and used for some time by the French resistance, the Maquis, during the German occupation. The Collet Chalet had been trashed and left in an appalling condition, and the Chalet itself, while not badly damaged, was in poor condition too. Jack and Teddy visited it briefly in 1946 to assess the damage, and again in 1947 and 1948, to clean up the Chalet and make some minor repairs. The Collet Chalet was judged impossible to salvage from its degraded condition, and with a heavy heart, as it had many fond memories for them, they arranged for it to be dismantled. The Chalet was put into a state that made it fit to occupy again, but at some point during these three years they decided that it would be too difficult to maintain as a regular summer holiday home, and began to look for a buyer. Despite some nibbles by prospective purchasers, however, no sale was forthcoming.

But before a family holiday at the Chalet could be organised, and following the end of his part-time appointment as county cadet commandant in August of 1948, family business in another continent beckoned. Teddy had already, in the autumn of 1946, paid a visit to Argentina in connection with the family's ranching business. In January 1949, both Jack and Teddy, accompanied this time by their wives, went on an extended trip of four months to visit the estancia and review its potential as a family asset; some ten years, as it happens, before its ultimate expropriation in 1959 by the provincial government.[2]

They sailed on both legs of the voyage by ocean liner, from Tilbury to Buenos Aires and back. Air travel for a purpose such as theirs was still a rarity, and the much more leisurely process of sea travel could be enjoyed without stress. They stayed for several weeks at the estancia, which was lived in by the British manager Robert Raikes, riding around the estate, playing pelota and climbing the local mountains. On the return voyage, Teddy was captivated by an attractive fellow passenger, an Argentinian lady who was the wife of the director of the Buenos Aires zoo, and who entertained him with stories of the various exotic animals at the zoo. He was particularly entranced with her account of the hatching of an iguana's eggs, and held forth about it more than once on his return to Morestead. Finally he reached for the appropriate volume of the *Encyclopaedia Britannica* to verify a point, and was considerably taken aback to find that it described the iguana as 'bringing forth its young alive' – much to the amusement of Joyce, who felt that he had been excessively taken with his new acquaintance.

This trip seems to have marked a turning point in his general health. Up to, and certainly during, his Argentine holiday, he had been spry and vigorous, still enjoying a number of active sports, but shortly afterwards his health declined.

2 Under Argentine inheritance law, title to the property passed down to all direct descendants of the original owner, their father Edward Norton, so that with each generation it became divided into a larger and larger number of smaller and smaller shares.

One result was that, on doctor's orders, he was unable to accompany his family on the long-planned summer holiday at the Chalet, which took place later in the same year. He was devastated that he could not personally introduce his sons to the place so near to his heart. To prepare us for the visit, he painted, from memory but with great accuracy of detail, a wonderful panorama of the valley of Les Fonds and the surrounding mountain ranges, an imaginary bird's-eye view. He used it to talk us through all his favourite spots and routes. Les Fonds and its environs were, to us newcomers, as delightful as their reputation. We returned there again in 1953, but again Teddy was forbidden by his doctor to come too, though he and Joyce did, later in that year, visit Dick, by now married and with a baby son, in West Germany – his last trip abroad.

To visit the Chalet in 1953 was again an enchanting experience. We climbed the highest mountain in the valley, the Buet, and gave rise to the quip about his trousers mentioned in an earlier chapter. Joyce recorded in the Chalet diary 'a wonderful spell of weather … a very successful holiday.' The Chalet remained on the market, but no buyers appeared. It was not until 1958 that it finally changed hands and passed out of the Norton family's ownership, bought by the Anglo-French Lucas family domiciled in Paris, whose property it remains to this day.

PASSING THE BATON

To revert to 1949, coinciding with the decline in his physical health, Teddy also began, at the age of sixty-five, to lose some of the sparkle and vigour characteristic of his earlier years, and his manner became more subdued. But, although he could no longer take part in the more active sports – in spite of which he continued fishing and shooting up to the year of his death – he applied himself to teaching his sons the whole range of activities that had given him so much pleasure throughout his life. This, in fact, became a major focus of his retirement years, both before and after his health took a turn for the worse.

To begin with, he personally coached us at cricket and tennis. He arranged riding lessons for us, and persevered to the point where we had learned that basic familiarity with horse management that is not forgotten in later life. Dick went much further, and became an accomplished horseman. Teddy's approach to horsemanship was not for the faint-hearted. 'You cannot call yourself a true horseman until you have fallen off ten times', he would say, and I began to keep count, with a sense of foreboding, of how many more times I would have to fall off before reaching that state of grace. I never got there. His efforts to interest us in mountains and mountaineering, on the other hand, fell on more fertile ground. Even the pleasures of simply walking in the countryside he taught us. The dogs that he kept during retirement gave plenty of excuse for this form of exercise.

He enthusiastically imparted his keen interest in natural history. Birdwatching and wildflower spotting were a constant theme. We would go on outings with him to count how many different bird species we could see in a day – a practice he had discovered, he told us, when trying to persuade his hard-of-hearing father that bird life had not completely vanished from his garden. In particular, he emphasised the importance of recognising bird calls and birdsong, which was a notable skill of his. He found in Bill a very apt pupil. He was forever displaying his interest in weather and climate, so that we grew up alert to weather phenomena and the seasons. He taught us butterfly collecting, which had not in those days become as unacceptable a hobby as it is now, both the skills of stalking and pouncing and those of killing and setting them well, so as to have a collection worthy of display. We learned the way to make a killing bottle by crushing laurel leaves, which give off a lethal gas, under blotting paper in a screw-top jar. Collecting butterflies helped us appreciate the amazing and complex beauty of their wing patterns and colours.

When it came to fishing, Joyce joined him as our tutor. They did their best to teach us fly fishing for trout and trolling for salmon – we were not the best of pupils. The only activity about which he failed entirely to enthuse his sons was shooting game birds; and indeed, by the time he tried, his eyesight was beginning to deteriorate, and he did not persevere when he saw our lack of interest.

Finally, he invested a lot of time in teaching us to draw and paint, though not, sadly, to learn his skills as a caricaturist. In addition to pencil sketching, watercolour and, to a lesser extent, body colour were his media. His preferred subject matter was landscape or still life. We would set off with our sketching stools and paraphernalia and seek good subjects in the surrounding villages, woods and fields (or mountains and lochs while in Scotland). Sometimes we were accompanied by his friend Colonel Nairne, a skilled amateur watercolourist whom we were encouraged to observe and learn from, for Teddy was much too disparaging about his own ability. We then compared results, and had post-mortem discussions about them. When it came to drawing, he invented ways to stimulate our imagination, such as declaring a competition to illustrate every line of 'The House that Jack Built', one day per line, a new winner to be declared each day.

Looking back on these years, I now realise the huge favour he did us by passing on those things that had enriched his own life. He was far from believing that it was the job of schools alone to teach his children games, sports, and how to make the most of their leisure time. Indeed, he thought that it was at least as important to teach them these things as the wherewithal to earn a living. For myself, I only remember a single occasion when he offered me any advice on what calling or profession to choose, and it was one (the law) that I elected not to follow. In the event, Bill in due course took up a career in the Civil Service, first as a diplomat and subsequently in the Treasury, while I became a businessman. I believe my father would have regarded this sequence of career choices, from soldiering in his eldest son through public service to commerce, as being in the appropriate order, and anyway it reflected our individual preferences.

It was during these later years that Joyce and Teddy were greatly saddened by the loss of her mother Violet Pasteur, whose quiet and charming life had lasted well into her eighties. She died in late September 1952, the last of our four grandparents and, in my case, the only one I had ever known.

NATURAL HISTORY

The second major focus of his retirement years was his detailed natural history notebooks. He kept these continuously, with at times almost daily entries, from September 1943 to May 1954. They were written in pencil (his military training having taught him that entries in ink would fade sooner) in his meticulously neat handwriting, in hard-backed notebooks with ruled lines and margins. The notes covered weather and seasonal observations, sightings or hearings of birds and birdsong – particularly the first arrival dates of spring migrants, of which he kept almost obsessively accurate records for many years – and the earliest dates of spring wildflowers coming into bloom.

He also recorded all and any observations that caught his naturalist's fancy. For instance, starting in May 1946, he observed a female blackbird feeding on the lawns at Morestead Grove with a distinctive crest caused by some ailment, which mated with an albino male. Their offspring inherited versions of these disabilities, and these unmistakeable individuals enabled him to study territorial behaviour in neighbouring breeding pairs of blackbirds over several years. He entered his sightings and conclusions patiently in the notebooks, and I later condensed them into an article that won a school competition. In April 1949 he made a note of the seven successive attempts by a robin to build a nest, almost all of them inside rooms in the house (*'we are besieged and cannot leave any windows on west side of the house open'*), before it finally succeeded, in May/June, in building and hatching in an outhouse.

His observations on weather make it clear that extremes of drought and heavy rainfall were as frequent then as in these days of climate change, and low winter temperatures with prolonged frosts were, of course, a lot more frequent. Apart from the late cold winter of 1946–1947, often cited among severe winters and remembered by older generations today, the winter of 1952–1953 included *'the worst last quarter I ever remember as regards weather'*, and on 16 March 1953 he noted there had been eighty-five nights of frost since October. On the other hand, there were severe droughts. In May 1949, *'phenomenally dry spring ... garden burnt to a cinder'*, and still in July *'unbroken drought continues ... garden a desert.'* And there was prolonged rainfall in the winter of 1950–1951, so much so that prayers for the rain to stop were offered in churches in March 1951, since *'the last six months have been a record wet period for all time – farmers in despair.'*

Alongside these catalogues of weather extremes, many entries convey his delight at what he sees or experiences. He recorded seventy-seven different species of wildflower on a two-mile walk from Twyford to Morestead in July 1948, and eighty-five over the same stretch in July 1953. His love of the spring bird migration, and sadness at its ending, comes across in the entry for 9 May 1952, *'Garden warbler at Morestead Grove ends the list of spring migrants for this year. Alas!'*

As with the sporting diaries from earlier phases of his life, he used the left-hand pages of the notebooks to record occasional items of interest unrelated to natural history. From the summer of 1952, these peripheral entries begin to reflect, in his laconic style, physical infirmities that caused him distress. They start in August 1952 with comments on his deteriorating eyesight; by December, '*my eyes have become useless to me as regards bird watching.*' Then in May 1953 he notes that his hearing for birdsong is letting him down. From June 1953 he begins to suffer, and record, minor arterial spasms, amounting to three in the space of eight months.

The entry for 12 May 1954 is typical of the varied range of his observations, '*Two perfect hot cloudless days with temperature up to 73 degrees daily and quite warm nights – hardly a cloud in the sky – copper beech burst into leaf – ground very parched – pigeons destroying vegetables. Tremendous run on birdbath. No more house martins since 9th – have been clearing up rockery and applying weed killer for last 3 days. Chestnut in full flower.*' The May 13th entry reads simply, '*Temperature 76 degrees y'day. Minimum 53 degrees. House martin prospecting again.*'

There the entries stop, and the rest of the notebook is blank.

THE END, AND THE LEGACY

On May 14th he was afflicted with a moderately severe stroke, which deprived him of speech, and much of the movement in his right arm and leg. Within a few days he was moved to a nursing home run by Joyce's brother-in-law. There he tried desperately to recover his speech and movement, and his frustration at not being able to convey the workings of his brain was painful to witness. I recall his obvious relief when, on a visit to his bedside, I was able to interpret a comment he was struggling to make about a watercolour painting that Bill, then living in Geneva, had sent him. After three and a half months he was fit enough to return to Morestead on September 1st, but was still much afflicted by the aftermath of the stroke. As it happened, I left home the following day on call-up into the gunners as an eighteen-year-old national serviceman. I saw him again briefly in October, when, in a spell of brilliantly fine late-summer weather, he sat out in the garden thoroughly enjoying the surroundings. His speech was slowly beginning to return.

In the last days of October he suffered a second, more serious stroke. He died in his bed at home a few evenings later on November 3rd, and Joyce entered on her long drawn-out widowhood. His death certificate gave as cause of death cerebral thrombosis and arteriosclerosis.

He was buried in a private ceremony on November 6th at Fareham, his old home town, in a family grave where his father had also been laid to rest. A memorial service was held at Winchester Cathedral on November 10th. The large congregation included representatives of the Royal Regiment of Artillery and its master gunner, the RA Association, the Royal Hampshire Regiment, the Home Guard (which had been re-formed twice since its disbandment in 1944), the Hampshire Army Cadet Force, the Territorial Army, the British Legion, the Alpine Club, the Royal Geographical Society, the Indian Mountain Artillery Old Comrades' Association, and, perhaps rather surprisingly, of Charterhouse School.

Obituaries, apart from those which featured in the national daily and local newspapers, appeared in the *Alpine Journal*, the *Himalayan Journal*, the *Geographical Journal*, the *Fell and Rock Climbing Club Journal*, the RA *Regimental News*, and *The Gunner*. Howard Somervell, always eloquent in print, wrote in the *Fell and Rock Climbing Club* obituary 'He would never wilfully hurt or offend anyone, nor would he ever let anyone down', and spoke in the *Alpine Journal* of 'his three chief characteristics – stability, humility and generosity'. About their time together on Everest, he wrote in *The Gunner*, 'In a large party of climbers, there are usually some who get on well with people, others who do not, and some who seem to make the rest get on well with one another – Norton was one of these last, always friendly and a centre of friendship'. In the *Himalayan Journal*, General Wilson wrote 'He was always scrupulously careful to ensure that no action of his should be in any degree unfair or ungenerous to others.' His old friend Alanbrooke summed him up thus in the RA *Regimental News*, 'Blessed with that rare gift of living intensely … he knew better than most how to combine work with pleasure while excelling in both.' And another old friend, Tom Longstaff, wrote in the *Alpine Journal*, 'Yet it is as the perfect companion that he is lamented, but remembered with joy.'

Joyce received, of course, many letters of condolence and sympathy. Here are some extracts that must have given her a great deal of comfort:

Humphrey Trevelyan:

> 'He was so genuinely interested in other people's doings; one
> of his many charming characteristics … I have learnt a
> lot from him, and so must many others have learnt from his
> wisdom, his strong yet gentle character and humour.'

Eric Shipton:

> 'Quite apart from his having been, naturally, a boyhood hero,
> General Norton was for so many of us a *beau idéal*, and I know
> of no one who commanded such universal respect and
> spontaneous affection.'

Ambrose Pratt:

> 'I once told Monty that E.F.N. were initials that meant more
> to generations of gunner subalterns than those of any
> other regimental leader. Kindness – humility – courage
> – understanding.'

H.V. Osborne, in a letter that came out of the blue to my mother:

> 'I had the privilege of being Battery Sergeant Major in the
> 21st Pack Battery at Norwich when the General was our
> Commanding Officer and I need hardly say we were a happy
> and efficient Battery. The Colonel as he was then was our
> counsellor and friend as well as our C.O.'

His painting companion Colonel Nairne:

> 'It has been a matter of the greatest pride to me to have
> known your General, and to have enjoyed his warm
> friendship. I admired him immensely – partly of course for
> his achievements, but more so for the amazing modesty
> with which he spoke of them.'

And Tom Longstaff again:

> 'He was my hero. The only man I can set beside my father
> in my affections.'

So ended Edward Felix Norton's life. A life lived at first in the high noon
of the British Empire, and then through its slow decline and twilight,
by one who was born fortunate, but who made the most of every
experience that his fortunate life offered. He evolved from an ebullient
young soldier and sportsman into a mature man of wide sympathies
and interests, with a talent for leadership that went far beyond mere
charisma. Ironically, his most striking and best-known achievement,
the two Everest expeditions of the 1920s and especially the second,
which he led, were an almost accidental digression from his lifetime

career as a soldier. His chief legacies, it could be argued, were the example he set to high-altitude mountaineers of what can be achieved at the extreme edge of human capability, and the many thousands of lives that he saved by the construction of air raid shelters in Hong Kong. But perhaps his true legacy was, as it still is, in the memories of those who knew him best: memories of him as a husband, father and friend, of the strong values that he believed in, 'his clear views of what's right and what's wrong', of his modesty, charm and generosity, and of his restless and untiring curiosity about the whole world around him.

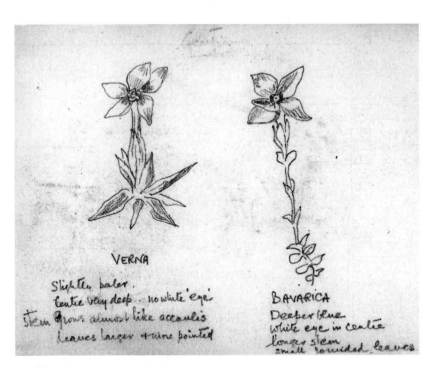

Alpine gentians.

TEDDY NORTON'S FAMILY TREE

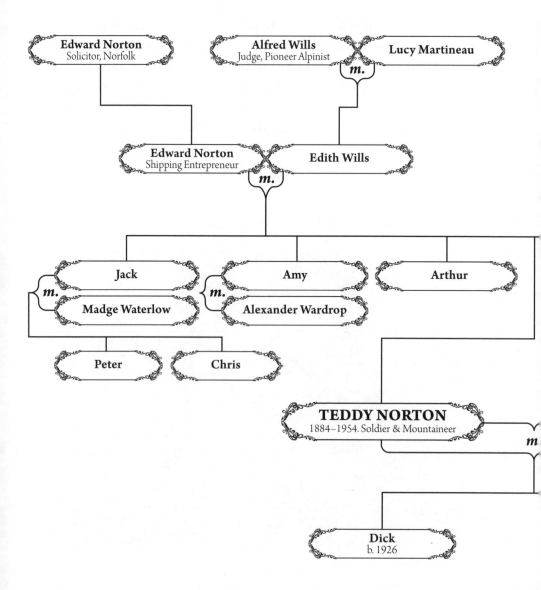

Edward Norton
Solicitor, Norfolk

Alfred Wills
Judge, Pioneer Alpinist

m.

Lucy Martineau

Edward Norton
Shipping Entrepreneur

m.

Edith Wills

m.

Jack

Madge Waterlow

m.

Amy

Alexander Wardrop

Arthur

Peter

Chris

TEDDY NORTON
1884–1954. Soldier & Mountaineer

m

Dick
b. 1926

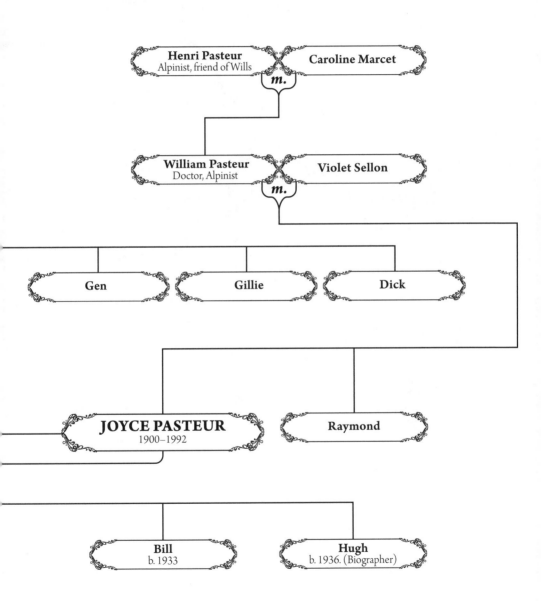

NOTE: The family tree is incomplete.
Only family members mentioned by name in the book are shown.

Henri Pasteur
Alpinist, friend of Wills

m.

Caroline Marcet

William Pasteur
Doctor, Alpinist

m.

Violet Sellon

Gen

Gillie

Dick

JOYCE PASTEUR
1900–1992

Raymond

Bill
b. 1933

Hugh
b. 1936. (Biographer)

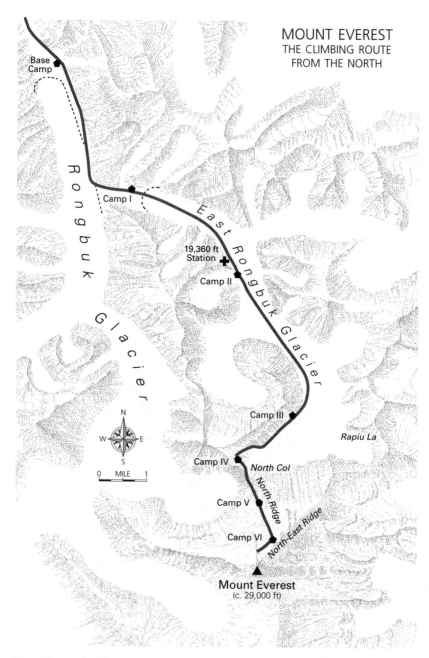

MOUNT EVEREST
THE CLIMBING ROUTE
FROM THE NORTH

Base
Camp

Rongbuk Glacier

Camp I

East Rongbuk Glacier

19,360 ft
Station

Camp II

Camp III

Rapiu La

Camp IV

North Col

N
W E
S

0 MILE 1

Camp V

North Ridge

Camp VI

North-East Ridge

Mount Everest
(c. 29,000 ft)

Mount Everest, the climbing route from the north. The 1922 expedition established Base
Camp and camps I–V; Camp VI was established by Norton and Somervell during the
1924 summit attempt.

India around 1900–1940 (now comprising India, Pakistan and Bangladesh).

ACKNOWLEDGEMENTS

My gratitude for the help I have received as an author goes in very large part, as I have said in the preface, to my brothers Dick and Bill, but many others have been supporters or advisers during the book's gestation. Special thanks go to my wife Joy for her unfailing encouragement and patience, and especially for her help with proofreading; to my nephew Christopher Norton for invaluable guidance through many aspects of the publishing process; to my sister-in-law Claire Harcup for commenting on drafts and for sharing her expert editorial knowledge, and her partner Michael Burdett for continuous encouragement and for help with sourcing illustrations; to my parents-in-law John and Mary Harcup for reading drafts and helping improve the text; to my cousin Tom Pasteur, who is now sadly no longer with us, and to Giles de la Mare for explaining the publisher's point of view; to Professor John West for his encouragement and for specialist insights into high-altitude physiology; and to the Royal Geographical Society, the Alpine Club, the British Library, the National Archive and the Imperial War Museum for access to their relevant archives, and especially to Glyn Hughes the honorary archivist of the Alpine Club, who was generous with his time.

Finally, I am very much indebted to Wade Davis – author of *Into the Silence*, the masterly account of the Everest expeditions of the 1920s – for agreeing to write the foreword to this book, and for doing so with such promptness and with such good grace.

My thanks go to the following persons and organisations for granting kind permission for use of photography and illustrations:

The National Portrait Gallery for the 1952 formal portrait of EFN.
The Liddell Hart Military Archive for images of Meerut and of WWI.
David Somervell for the image of EFN seated during his 1924 high climb.
Sandra Noel and the Royal Geographical Society for the image of EFN on his high climb with the summit of Everest beyond him.
Rob Norton for two black and white images and one colour image.
The Norton Everest Archive for the EFN's Everest sketches and certain other images mostly specific to Everest.
Vertebrate Publishing for two of the three maps in the appendices.